# THE IMPORTANCE OF BEING KENNEDY'S

---

## THE FLYNNS BOOK FIVE

## KAYT MILLER

# THE FLYNN FAMILY

5

## THE IMPORTANCE OF BEING KENNEDY'S

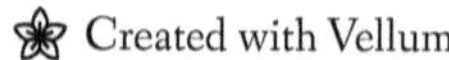 Created with Vellum

CONTENTS

FROM THE DESK OF ERNEST FLYNN

---

**Dear Chick Who's Reading This Shit,**
*(Or dude. No judgment here, man.)*

I'm irritated. The book before this one was supposed to be all about me, but my asshat baby brother ended up stealing the show. So, this little book is all about me—about me getting my shit together, about me figuring out that Kennedy Corcoran's my girl, and about me working my ass off to convince that same Kennedy Corcoran that I'm her man. It hasn't been easy because my woman is stubborn. And bossy. Oh, and dominant. Surprisingly, I've discovered the dominant side of my girl is hot as hell. But more about that later.

So, sit tight and enjoy the ride, and don't expect to hear word one about my little brother. Well, not much anyway. I'm sure he'll get his nose in my business because he's a dick like that.

I'm out.

    E.

---

# PROLOGUE: A LITTLE BACKGROUND

## ERNIE

All right, for those of you out there who didn't read the book that was *supposed* to be about me, let me give you the lowdown. (Deep breath here.) I used to live with my best friend, Hammer-Time. Okay, her name is Hammer, Claire Hammer—more specifically, Mary Claire Hammer. For years, I called her Hammer or any derivative of an M.C. Hammer song. Turns out she hated that. *Who knew?*

We met in college, both of us computer nerds. She was into game design, and I was into programming and everything related to that. I ended up getting a degree in data engineering. What's that? According to Google, *a data engineer is usually a data infrastructure engineer and is responsible for building and maintaining the software infrastructure that enables computation over large data sets.* Well, hell, I could have said that. I thought Google would dumb it down a little bit. It's pretty technical stuff for the average person to get.

No offense. Anyway, Hammer and I met a little over six years ago. When we graduated, we moved to Chicago together. I grew up in Chi-town; my family is all here, so the move was easy for me while Claire's from small-town Iowa. Anyway, I got us this apartment, and we lived together until shit hit the fan. After two long years of cohabitating with my best friend, she freaked out on me and moved out one night and in with my little brother, Ethan.

Ugh, *Ethan*. The douche. He loved that she left me and moved in with him. He'd been practically salivating to get his hands on Claire since he was sixteen. He claims it was love at first sight or some bullshit like that. Okay, well, I may not be as cynical about that love shit as I used to be. But you'll have to wait a little longer to hear about that.

Anyway, when she left, I honestly thought my life was ending. Not because I had feelings for her. It was because she was the only person that got me. She understood I had issues like a fear of meeting new people and some other social anxiety issues. Claire always had my back. She took care of me. Claire took care of *everything*.

After she moved out, it messed with my head and flipped my world upside down. To give you a little taste of the destruction she caused, during the time my *supposed* best friend ignored me, I got sick, lost my job, ate my weight in frozen pizza, drank an equal amount of beer and Irish whiskey, forgot how to clean up after myself or shower, gained thirty pounds—essentially, hitting rock bottom. There was an intervention, of sorts, when my brother Ed begged Claire to try to pull me out of my pit of despair.

She did help, a little. That is until I fucked her on my couch and snuck away from her in the night to get into my big, warm, comfy bed, leaving her on the couch without a blanket, uh, or clothes—not the most gentlemanly thing to do. Live and learn.

Hooking up with Claire was a fucking disaster. The sex was good, sure. It was weird, though. It was kind of like sleeping with a stepsister or something. Good but wrong. Know what I mean? I don't think she was that excited to repeat the act either.

She wouldn't reply to any text messages or calls afterward. She totally ghosted me for weeks.

Things slowly got better after I had a literal meltdown one day at my doctor's office. I went to see Dr. Merkle after Ethan beat the shit out of me. Don't worry, I deserved it. I got my licks in on him too, so we're all good now. I had a broken nose, some busted fingers, a sprained wrist, and a few other bumps and bruises all over the rest of me. Honestly, I think I needed to get the shit beat out of me to knock some sense into me. That and in the waiting room, I sat next to a little girl whom I'd met on a previous visit. Her name is Ashley, and she has fucking cancer. She's around six years old, I'd guess. God, she's a beautiful little girl with huge smiling eyes and the biggest balls in the world.

That little pip-squeak is brave as fuck. With a scarf on her head and a mask over her mouth, she showed me such compassion by loaning me her precious fuzzy bear she called "Claire Bear" (no relation to my own Claire.) so I wouldn't be scared when I went in to see my doctor. That act was the single most kind and generous thing anyone has ever done for me. So, I lost it—literally and figuratively. I left the office after getting patched up and drove my car around aimlessly, or so I thought. It wasn't aimless at all because I ended up at my mom's grave— a place I hadn't been in eighteen years. I sat on the ground next to her and cried like a little bitch. I also talked to her. I told her all about my life, my successes, and my many, many failures. She listened because what the fuck else would she do?

In all seriousness though, I know my mom is always there for Dad, Ed, me, and even Ethan. My mom, Rachel Ann Flynn, died of cancer in her early thirties—way too fucking young. Dad always told us she was an angel on our shoulder, and thinking about her like that always helped.

Intellectually, I know she didn't want to leave me. But when you're seven, thinking about something like death in abstract terms like that is difficult. Seven-year-old Ernie thought she left him. Hell, twenty-five-year-old Ernie still felt that way. All it took was a six-year-old girl fighting for her little life and her determined mom to help me see things differently.

I think about Ashley now and then. That day at the doctor's office? Things didn't sound good for little Ashley. Her mom stood outside Ashley's exam room barely holding it together. She shook her head at me as I gave her a hug. Damn. It fucking tears me up thinking about the two of them. I prayed for her that day. I don't pray. But that little girl needed it, so I decided to think about someone other than myself for a change.

That new way of thinking extended into other parts of my life too. I reached out to Claire, apologizing for hurting her and for continually calling her Hammer-head, Claw, Ball-peen, and other clever hammer-related names. I also called my former assistant, Danika. She and I had a hate-hate relationship after I dissed her in front of the entire company (my old job) one day. She made my life a living hell afterward, so we're even. When I got canned, er, I mean resigned, she was laid off too. That sucked for her, but, like my usual M.O., I only cared about myself. So, after my cathartic afternoon at the doctor and the cemetery, I called her.

I think she was expecting my usual bullshit, so when I apologized, she was pretty shocked. She told me she got a job as a recruiter for a tech company in the city and that she was much happier. When she asked me if I was looking for a gig, I was fucking floored. "Yeah, I'm not working yet," I confessed to her.

"Well, we've got an opening doing pretty much what you did before. You interested?"

"Hell yeah," I said exuberantly into the phone. "That's cool of you, Danika."

"Yeah, well, I'm pretty awesome. It's too bad you never saw that, you douche."

I hung up with her at that point, laughing. A short time later, I had an interview for the following day, and I was an official CompuTech employee by the end of the interview. I'd love to tell you that I lived happily ever after at CompuTech, but that'd be a bald-faced lie.

1

---

## MEETING A SHE-DEVIL NAMED KENNY

ERNIE

It's official. I'm no longer a data engineer. I'm now a construction apprentice. The first one sounds way cooler, but in reality, that job sucked. CompuTech was pissed as hell that I quit after three weeks and four days, but whatever. I offered to give them two weeks' notice, but they told me to get my stuff and go. Fine by me.

Today's my first day at Flynn Construction. My older brother, Ed, told me to head to their big commercial project and report to the foreman, Kenny, at eight in the morning. At eight twenty, I pull into the site and park next to a bunch of dirty old pickups and rusty cars. I hesitate to leave my baby in the lot next to these jalopies, but I've got to hurry my ass up. I'm already late. My wait at Mickey D's was extra long.

I slide out of my car, making sure not to ding my door on the red rust-bucket next to me. I grab my ball cap, thermos, and cooler that holds my lunch and some sodas inside. I walk around some scraps of lumber, jump over a couple of concrete blocks, and make my way over to a guy reading some sort of architectural plan. "Kenny?"

The guy doesn't even look up. He points behind him. "Back there. Plaid shirt."

"Thanks." I look behind him and see the back of a short, fat little dude. He's got on a red, plaid flannel shirt tucked into heavy duty work pants that are a couple sizes too big in the ass and are cuffed at the ankles about four inches. Dude's short. "Jesus, that guy's the foreman?" I say under my breath. "He's out of shape. Probaby can't do much."

I walk up toward the guy, and when I get about twenty feet away, I say, "Kenny?" I stop moving as soon as he starts to turn around. Slowly stepping toward me, Kenny removes the hard hat, and my breath catches in my throat. Held at bay by that white construction helmet is the reddest, wildest mass of curls I've ever seen. The curls descended into a long wild braid that plopped down out of the helmet onto Kenny's shoulder.

My mouth agape, I look from the hair to the face then down to the shirt. Kenny slowly walks toward me. "Well, well, well, you must be Ernest. It's *soooo* nice of you to join us this morning. Did you have car trouble or something?"

*It's a trap.* Kenny's voice sounds nice—sweet, actually, but her face? It looks pissed. I clear my throat. "You're a chick."

"Oh, wow," she says, putting her finger on her chin, tapping it, "I heard you were some kind of genius, but seeing it firsthand *is* pretty amazing. What gave it away?"

I look down at her chest then back up to her face. "Uh, your tits. They're huge."

Her face, freckled and plump, has turned fire-engine red. *Uh-oh. I shouldn't have said that.* Her golden-brown eyes have turned into glowing golden orbs. Honestly, the visual of everything together is breathtaking. Kenny is fucking glorious when she's pissed.

My eyes are trained on hers as she slowly gets closer and closer to me until her tits are up against my abs. Funny, a month ago I'd have called those my big *belly*, but I've worked my ass off to lose the weight after my, how shall we say, hiatus from work. Instead of going to a job every day, I ate frozen pizza and drank beer while sitting on my ass for the better part of three months. So, yeah, anyway, I look down and watch them, Kenny's tits, as they make contact. My dick twitches in my pants, and it surprises me. Damn! *Fat chicks don't usually arouse me.*

I look back up at her face then at her hand. She's giving me the come-hither motion with her finger. I guess she wants me to bend down. I bend for what seems like forever until our faces are about three inches apart. This close I can smell her. She's sweet, like sugar cookies. I fucking love sugar cookies. I can also see her face close-up. She's not wearing any makeup. She doesn't need to. Her skin is perfect. There's not a blemish in sight. She's got long auburn eyelashes and freckles all over the bridge of her nose and on her cheeks. Another thing, she can't be more than five feet soaking wet. I'm nearly bent in half. My observations are interrupted when she grasps me by the T-shirt. I'm a little worried she's going to try to kiss me in front of everyone. *Hell no, not gonna happen.* But she surprises me. Instead of trying to lay one on me, she speaks quietly, saying, "Ernest Flynn?"

"Uh, yeah?"

"You're fired." She lets go of my shirt, turns, and marches back to her original spot.

Huh? "Uh, you can't fire me. My dad—"

She whips back around to face me. "I know who your fucking dad is, you asshole. I told him I didn't want you on my crew. I've heard enough stories about you to know you're a self-important douche. I don't need you, and I don't want you. You may show yourself out," she says, giving me that sweeping hand gesture. Like I'm dirt.

"You didn't even give me a chance, Kenny."

"You're thirty minutes late. You had your chance; you fucking blew it. Now go. You're wasting my valuable time."

I snort then scoff. "Your valuable time?" I chortle. "What'd you do to get this gig, fuck Ed?" I start to laugh, but when I see her face, I know I said the wrong thing. She's going to kill me. She's got a hammer in her belt, and she's reaching for it. She walks to me slowly again, like a panther does before it rips the jugular from its prey.

I back up a couple of steps, keeping my eye on her hand. She reaches slowly into her belt to pull out a cell phone. I audibly sigh in relief. That is until I hear these words: "Donal? It's Kennedy. He was late, he's an asshole, and I fired his ass. Stick him somewhere else."

My eyes must be huge because she smirks at me as she listens to my dad. The smirk turns to a scowl then to an eye roll. She hands me her phone. "Here!"

She turns and walks back to her spot. I put the phone to my ear. "Yeah?"

"Fired on the first fucking day, son?" Dad usually doesn't cuss unless he's super pissed.

"I had car tro—"

"You drive an Audi. Enough with the bullshit car problems. Why were you late? Tell me the fucking truth."

I mumble out the words as fast as I can, "Thelinewassuperlongatmickyd's."

"The drive through was busy? Is that what you're saying to me, son? You're late because you had to get something to eat?"

"And coffee."

"You're too soft, boy You need this job. You need to work up a damn sweat. You need hard, physical labor."

"No, I don't. I thought I was here to learn the business."

"Ha!" Dad laughs. "I told you you'd be starting at the

bottom. Now let me talk to Kenny. I'll see if I can talk her into giving you another chance."

"But, Dad," I whisper into the phone, "she's a chick."

"What?" Dad feigns shock. "Are you serious? Kenny's a girl?"

I whisper again, "Yeah. She's got tits. *Big ones.*"

"I hope to fuck you didn't say that to her."

Silence.

"Jesus, Ernie. You can't talk to women like that in the workplace. Hell, anywhere. Have some fucking class."

"Class. Got it." I laugh at my own joke, but Dad isn't laughing.

"Let me talk to her. You'd better hope she gives you another shot."

I'm not sure I want another shot. Working for a girl on a construction site? No thanks. Sighing, I sit on a pile of lumber and rest my face in my palm and watch her as she fumes on the phone with my dad. "Damn, she's a spitfire," I mutter to myself. She's pacing around back and forth, moving her free hand around like she's using it to emphasize her point, but she's wasting her energy. Dad can't see her doing that.

She moves pretty damn fast for a bigger girl. In no time, she's gone from her original spot over to an area next to a trencher. She puts her phone against her chest and yells at a kid standing up on the second level on nothing but a two-by-four. "Yo, Cherry. Get your fucking ass off that board and get down here."

"What? Why?" the kid whines. He can't be much older than eighteen or nineteen.

"*Don't* question me, Cherry. You're being unsafe, which makes my site unsafe for others around you. You've got two fucking seconds to get down here, or you're fucking fired."

The guy she calls "Cherry" teeters a bit and nearly falls.

He's not wearing a hard hat, and when he starts to wobble, another guy reaches out to grab him and almost falls himself.

"See? Jesus, you almost caused Dave to fall. Get. Down. Here!" she says, pointing to the spot at her feet.

"Yes, ma-ma'am," the kid stutters.

Placing the phone back to her ear she says, "Fuck my life. I'm not a goddamn babysitter, Don." She's quiet as she listens to Dad. "Fine. I'll give him one more chance." She's looking at me now, holding up one finger. The middle one. "That's it though, Don. That's it."

She ends the call and sticks her phone back into her belt as Cherry approaches her. She puts her arm around him and pulls him close. I can't hear her, but I'm watching the kid's face. Her lips haven't stopped moving, and when I see tears dripping onto the kid's gray tee, I'm mesmerized. "What the fuck did she say to him?"

"Probably gave him the 'You're a man now, so grow a pair' speech. It's a good one. Makes me cry every time I hear it." I turn to see who said that. It's a guy about my dad's age strolling by with his cooler. I expect him to laugh at his own joke, but he doesn't. He arches his brow and nods. "Seriously, it's pretty empowering. Lucky little fucker, that Cherry."

"Cherry? That's his name?"

The man chuckles. "No, Cherry. That's what we call the new guys." He laughs as he walks toward a long white trailer.

"Great."

2

## I FEEL LIKE I'M GONNA DIE

### ERNIE

"What a fucking day," I groan as I step out of my car. I turn to grasp my small cooler and wince. My body hurts in places I didn't know could hurt. Has the back of your knees ever hurt? Mine either. At least not until today. Gingerly, I pull the front door of my building open. Inside, I look at the stairs and nearly weep. I live four floors up, and there's no elevator. The only way I'm going to make it up is on my hands and knees.

It takes me at least twenty minutes to get to my apartment door. Putting the key in the lock is nearly impossible since I can't hold my arm up long enough to insert the damn key. When I finally get it, I stumble in and fall face-first onto my sofa. I'm dirty, tired, and hungry. "I wish Hammer were here."

I reach into my back pocket and grab my phone. Locating her number, I hit Send.

"Hello? Ernie?" Claire says, a little too casually for my current state of pain.

"Help!"

"Ernie! What's wrong? Are you hurt?"

"Yes. New job. Hurt me. Need food. Water. You. Help Ernie!"

Claire giggles on her end of the phone. "Poor baby. Want me to come over with some food?"

"Yes, please."

"Can I bring your brother? He can help you get to the shower."

"Yes, please."

"Okay. We'll be there soon."

"Hurry. Fading fast."

I listen to her giggle as she hangs up. God, I'm so glad I got my friend back. "Now if I could only exorcise the fucking demon named Kenny I work for, then I'd be set." She's a damn she-devil. She had me shoveling dirt from eight forty-five until five thirty. I had to work an extra thirty minutes after everyone else left to make up for being "tardy." Her words.

*Yeah, well, her words suck.*

She sat on her big ass and watched me dig those last thirty minutes, pointing out everything I was doing wrong. *"Don't lift with your back. You're gonna get hurt. Scoop in a pendulum motion, it's easier."*

Blah, blah, blah. God, she's fucking Satan. That is if Satan were a fiery redhead, which, come to think about it, I'm sure he is. Jesus, I'm delirious. "Hurry, Claire. I'm not gonna last much longer."

I wake up to pounding. I raise my head about two inches off the couch and want to scream in pain. Instead, I croak, "It's open." I watch the door open and hope like fuck it's not home invaders because I wouldn't be able to defend myself.

"Hey, Ernie," Ethan says, slapping me on the back.

I yelp in pain. "Ouch, fucker."

"Claire's gonna make you some food. I'm gonna help you get into the shower."

"Cool."

Ethan helps me up, and I nearly pass out by the time he's got me under the hot spray of water. "Wow, your bathroom looks great. Who cleaned it?"

"Maid to Clean." Yeah, so one of the things that happened when I was gainfully unemployed and depressed as fuck was my apartment didn't get very clean. Maybe "very clean" is an understatement. It was so bad in here, Dad made me hire someone to come in and give it a thorough cleaning. The place I called, Maid to Clean, had to wear hazmat suits and use special toxic waste bags to clean the bathroom. Apparently, mold is bad. Anyway, it's clean now and that's all that matters.

"Cool. Okay. I'll be out there helping Claire. Yell if you fall and you can't get up." He chuckles as he leaves.

"Har dee fucking har har." I stop speaking as soon as I step under the spray. *It feels so good; I could stay here forever.*

Wincing as I step out, I grab my towel, dry off, and reach for my clothes. When I find none, I look around my bathroom and see a fresh set of comfy stuff in their place. I slip on my tee, boxers, and those fucking hideous beer sleep pants my cousin Mick gave to all of us. "Stupid," I mutter while getting dressed. "At least they're comfortable."

Stepping out into the hallway I hear Claire. "He's alive!"

"Barely. Is the food ready?"

"It is."

I waddle to the couch and sit in my spot, wincing as I lower myself onto the seat. Claire's pulled out an old TV tray, circa 1975, from the front closet. On it is a bowl of tomato soup, crackers, and two grilled cheese sandwiches that are made on some pretty fancy bread.

"Wow, Hammer. This looks great." Looking around for their food I ask, "You're not eating?"

"Nah, we're going out. Celebrating," says my brother as he gazes at Claire.

"Celebrating what?" It's then that I notice the dress Hammer's wearing. It's black and short and low cut. She looks kind of sexy, if you like nerdy chicks. I look over at Ethan, and he's got on slacks and a dress shirt. No tie. He'll pass.

"Namely a new deal with Nerdovision," answers Ethan.

"New deal?"

"Yeah, when I turned them down the first time, they renegotiated the contract," Claire says, beaming.

"What's new about this one?" Her other contract was pretty amazing. They were going to pay her a substantial lump sum plus royalties from the game. On top of that, they wanted her to work for them, so she'd have salary and benefits on top of everything else. She didn't want to leave my dumb-ass brother, though, since he landed a job here in Chicago at that Steppenwolf Theater where he interned last summer.

"This deal lets me stay here most of the time. I'll fly out to San Francisco once a month, max."

"Same money and shit?"

"Pretty much," says Claire cryptically. "Maybe a little more. I've got a new game in the works. They like it even better than *The Bully Brigade.*"

"Awesome. So, does that mean I'm off the hook for the rent?"

"Hey, asswipe, you need to pay her back!" my brother says, jumping into the conversation.

"Just put it into a trust for our kids," Claire says, shocking me.

I look down at her now flat belly and then up to her face.

"No. Not pregnant." She smiles.

"Yet," says Ethan, smirking.

Whoa, that's pretty serious shit. Ethan and Claire with a

kid. Interesting. After wolfing down one delicious grilled cheese, I start on the second one. "Damn, woman. Great food."

"New recipe. I used sourdough bread and sharp white cheddar cheese." She turns and blushes at my bro.

Whatever that means. I'm not going to ask, because my guess is it's dirty. Something to do with melted cheese. I shiver imagining it. The burns alone would turn me off. Probably.

"Amazing," I say with my mouth full.

"So," Ethan starts, "which job do they have you on?"

"The big commercial site."

Ethan chuckles. "With Kenny?"

I groan so loud the neighbors could hear. "She's the *devil*."

Ethan laughs again. "She's not the devil. She knows her shit and doesn't put up with any bullshit."

I grunt as I eat a bite of sandwich I've dipped in the soup. Mm, so good. "She had me shoveling all fucking day long."

"You must have pissed her off."

"Were you late?" interjects Claire. She knows I have a problem with tardiness.

"Maybe."

"Don't be late, dude. She'll fire your ass."

"Well aware." I take another bite. "I don't get it. Why would they hire her? She's a girl, and she's pretty fat."

Claire gasps then stammers, "Don't you dare go there, Ernie. You hated it when everyone made fun of you after you'd gained weight. Just because you've lost some of it doesn't give you the right to say such mean things. She must be very good at her job."

I snort. "Sorry. I'll keep my thoughts to myself about Kenny." Actually, I'm gonna try to keep my thoughts about Kenny to a minimum. I found myself staring at her at weird times today. She's oddly attractive, if you like that kind of thing.

"Dude," my bro says with a laugh. "You don't remember her? Kennedy Corcoran?"

"No. Why should I?"

"She was in your class in high school for starters."

"She was?"

"Yeah, she ran with the popular crowd. You were with the other nerds, remember?"

I scoff. "She was popular?"

"Uh, yeah. She was on the homecoming court, student council, and a whole bunch of other shit."

"Homecoming? She must have been a lot smaller back then."

"Ernie!" Claire shouts.

"What? I'm serious." I shrug.

Ethan puts his arm around Claire as he says, "No, she looked pretty much the same except she used to make her hair flat back then. Now she lets it go all curly and shit."

She sure does. It's a shame her hair was covered by her hard hat most of the day. I'd have liked to get a glimpse of that wild mane again. It was shiny when the sun hit it. I wonder if it's soft.

"Dude? You with me?" asks Ethan.

"Yeah, tired. I've got four more days of Kenny's torture this week."

"Well, good luck to you," Ethan says, slapping my back. "We need to get going, or we'll be late for our reservation."

"Okay. Thanks, Claire. Talk to you later?"

"Sure thing, bestie."

I watch Ethan's face scrunch up at the sound of that word. I love it that it pisses him off that Hammer and I are friends again. He's gonna have to get used to it because I'm in it for the long haul with her. *The long-ass haul.*

# I'M PRETTY SURE THE GODS HATE ME

## KENNEDY

F ML.

For those of you out there who aren't well versed on text slang, FML means "Fuck My Life." If you're wondering why I'd start my chapter off with those three little words, it's because I think I'm going to pull my damn hair out with these new fucking cherries that Donal Flynn has saddled me with.

Case in point... "Cherry! What the fuck are you doing?" The particular cherry I'm yelling at now is called Tim in real life. In Kenny-land, he's Cherry #1. When he ignores me, pretending he can't hear me, I try again. "Now! Get your fucking ass over here, now!" I swear if I have to count to three to get him to listen, I'm walking off this site, getting into my truck, and I'm leaving. For good this time.

"Y-Yes, Kenny?"

Finally. Sighing, I say more quietly, "How many times do I have to tell you to wear your goddamn construction hat? It's a code violation for you to be on a site without your safety gear. Do you want this site shut down?"

"N-No."

"Do you want Donal and Declan to get fined?"

"N-No."

"Then put your fucking hat on."

"B-But they drew all over it."

*Jesus*, these guys always pull this shit. "So, get something and clean it off. You can't be on the site without your gear, Cherry."

"I thought you'd stop calling me Cherry when Ernie started."

"Well, *Cherry*"—I emphasize Cherry—"if you wouldn't pull shit like not wearing safety gear on the jobsite, I'd stop. But every fucking day, I've got to remind you about something, Jesus, Cherry. Get your shit together!"

I watch his eyes shimmer with unshed tears. *FML*. I swear I've made this kid cry a million times. It tugs on my damn heartstrings—a little—okay, not at all. But it *would* pain me a lot more if he actually got hurt. "Safety first, Timmy." There, I said his name. That'll make him happy.

"Tim. It's just Tim."

"Don't press your luck," I say, pissed again.

"Timmy's good. I'll take Timmy."

"Get your helmet and get back to work. If I see you without it again, I'll send you home. For good. Got it?"

"Got it, ma'am. Thank you."

*Ma'am?* I fucking hate being called *ma'am*. I'm only twenty-five.

"Good. Get back to work." I watch him walk over to the spot where everyone throws their shit in the morning. He pulls out his bright yellow helmet, and I have to put my hand over my mouth to keep from laughing. "Those assholes." They've drawn a tiara on the front of the thing and then written all sorts of stupid shit all over it relating to his cherry status—words like cherry, pussy, virgin, and I think there's a dirty limerick on the back. I'm positive Dave's responsible, but I'm not gonna call him out in front of everyone, yet. I want to wait until he does the same to Cherry #2—the real reason my life is fucked.

Ernest Flynn. *Ugh.* Where do I start with him? Maybe with the fact that a nerd has no business on a construction site. Then, I'll move onto the fact that this nerd hasn't done physical labor since he was a damn teen. Sure, he works out, that's obvious. His arms and back look, uh, like he's not averse to lifting weights. His abs are a little flabby, no doubt caused by too much beer or something. Don't get me wrong; I know I'm not a skinny Minnie, but I like my body. I'm sexy. I know it, and the guys I choose to take to my bed know it.

But I digress. Ernie Flynn is a problem. Whenever I tell him what to do, he looks at me like he wants to kill me. *Tough shit.* Donal said he needed to start at the bottom, so he's starting at the bottom. Shoveling is the first rung on the ladder. Shit, I had to do it. I shoveled dirt for weeks before my dad let me do anything else. It's the way it goes. He's going to have to man up if he plans on doing this job.

I'm pulled from my thoughts by the sounds of someone whining. Sure, these guys complain all the time. This voice is new, though. I walk around the side to the dig site and see Ernie bending at the waist, big hands on his thick thighs. "What's wrong now, Cherry?"

Without moving his big body, his head jerks up. "This is fucking bullshit, *Kenny*." He practically spits my name out. "I shouldn't have to dig like a common laborer."

"Well, here's the thing, *genius*, you *are* a common laborer."

"I'm—"

I put my fists up to my eyes like a baby does when they cry. "Poor Ernest." I pretend to sob. Jamming my hands on my hips again, I ask, "You think you're better than us?"

"No, I—"

"Because we all started right there," I say, pointing to the trench he's standing in.

"You didn't—"

"The fuck I didn't. I dug for three weeks before my dad let me do something else. Dave over there," I say, using my thumb to point behind me, "dug for weeks too. Johnny-cake, same thing." I put my hands back on my hips. "And to think, I was going to do you a favor and let you move up after a week, but now? That's not gonna happen, Cherry."

"What? Why not?" he says, dropping the shovel to the ground. The clanging sound rings out and draws everyone's attention to the scene in the trench.

"Because, Ernest, you need to learn, once and for all, that *I'm* in charge."

Ernie makes a scoffing noise, and I nearly come unglued. I hop down into the trench and step toward him slowly. I like to do that real slow to let them see how pissed I am. I get close enough until he can see the whites of my eyes. I draw in air, which is a mistake. I can smell him. He's all clean sweat and yummy man-soap. Shaking my head, I say, "I told you yesterday, Ernest." I look up and see he's bent down to get closer to me. I'm a little disarmed by his move, but I hold my ground. "You had one more shot. Your daddy isn't going to save you again, *precious.*"

He stays put, blinking a few times. "I'm not going to dig for weeks, *Kenny.*"

"You will if I tell you to, *Cherry.* Now get back to fucking work. Use your legs. You're fucking up your back doing it your way." I turn and stomp to the edge of the trench. With one hand, I place it on the edge of the pit and push up, and in one move, I'm up on my feet on level ground. I turn back to see Ernie staring at me, mouth agape. Picking up his shovel, he snorts like a damn bull and gets back to work. "Use your legs," I shout.

"I know!" he shouts without looking back. "Jesus!"

His little outburst makes me laugh, and I continue to do so until I get back to work. "Fuck. He's stubborn." It's going to take extra time with him. Hopefully, he won't screw this up, because if he's anything like Donal or Declan or the other Flynns who work here, he'll be good at this job.

## I MEAN IT. I HATE HER

### ERNIE

I survived. I lived through week one of Kenny Corcoran hell. The woman is frustrating. She's irritating. She struts around the place like she owns it. And bossy? She's fucking bossy as hell. I've never seen anything like it. Then there's the crew. They run around the site like she's the fucking Queen of Sheba. Or maybe it's Cleopatra. Whatever, it doesn't matter; they're both the same kind of chick. Everything is her way or the highway.

I don't get it, though. Watching her work, bitching at everyone, commanding them, it makes my dick hard as a fucking rock. Then Tuesday night I had a dream about her. I had one on Wednesday night and last night too. In the dreams, she stands with her hands on her big hips, demanding I do shit to her like, "Get on your knees, servant boy," "Fuck me, slave," and my personal favorite, "Lick my pussy, drudge."

In every dream, her hair is all unbraided and fucking wild. Her eyes practically glow with lust for me too. They're the hottest fucking dreams I've ever had. Hell, I've never even seen porn as hot as these dreams. I know they're just dreams. They don't mean that I'm suddenly hot for a big girl. It's caused by exhaustion, plain and simple. She works me like a damn mule, and I'm delirious. Yeah, that's all it is. Delirium.

The problem with that theory is that, in the light of day, I still can't stop thinking about her. Shoveling up a scoop of dirt, I wonder what she looks like naked. Tossing the dirt behind me, I imagine what it'd feel like sinking my big cock into that tight little pussy. "Oh, God," I look up and moan as I bend at the waist, attempting to keep my work pants from tenting. She's bending over the blueprints enough for me to see a little thong peeking out above her dirty old jeans. It's pink. The thong. It's hot fucking, pink. "Jesus." I'm so screwed.

"You got it bad for her, don't you, son?" says the old guy I talked to the first day as he stands on the edge of the fucking swimming-pool-size hole I'm working on. His name's John, but everyone calls him Johnny-cake for some odd reason.

"No!" I say way too loudly.

Johnny-cake chuckles. "Sure, Cherry. Whatever you say. But I will say this. You look at Kenny over there like I used to look at Mrs. Johnny-cake—with lust in my eyes. Forty years later, and I still can't get enough of her."

"Ooh, gross. I don't want to hear about you having old people sex, J.C." I've taken to shortening the whole "Johnny-cake" thing to two initials. It's easier.

J.C. throws his head back and laughs. "Suit yourself. But I'll tell you this, my woman's pussy is still the best thing this side of the Mississippi. Maybe the other side too." He pats my back and walks back to his work zone.

"Gross." I shiver.

"What's gross? Your face?"

Fucking Kenny. "Ha, ha. Very funny." I look up at her from the pit of despair. It's what I've named my personal work site. "What do you want? Can't you see I'm digging here?"

"Lunch," she mutters as she walks away. I watch her ass the

entire way. It's half covered by a flannel shirt, but I see enough to know that it's round and perky.

I crawl out of the hole, ending up on my hands and knees. Groaning as I push myself to stand, I walk toward the pile of coolers. Taking a seat on a stack of wood, I open my lunch box and peer inside. "I need to buy some better shit for lunch." All I've been eating this week is PB&J on white bread and granola bars. It's not enough food for the number of calories I've been burning off. I pat my stomach and can tell it's helping that part of me. I wish I had the energy at night to do some crunches, but I think the movements associated with shoveling are close to that kind of workout. Lost in thought, I don't realize Kenny has taken a seat across from me on a stack of concrete blocks.

I look up and watch her pull her lunch from a stainless-steel cooler. She's got a beautiful sandwich on a thick hoagie bun. It looks like roast beef with a ton of veggies and shit on it. She's also got a bag of potato chips, banana, pudding, carrots, a big bottle of water, and an enormous fucking cookie. I salivate at the sight of her food. I watch her unwrap the long hoagie then stare as she places the sub up to her mouth. Opening those lips wide, she takes a big bite and moans. Holy fuck, my dick! *Behave!* I say in my head. The truth is I've spent so much time looking at her hair, eyes, and ass that I've neglected that mouth of hers. Maybe it's because it's always spewing out vitriol.

Now that I've got a glimpse of it biting down on a sandwich about the same size as my dick, her lips mesmerize me. They're plump like the rest of her. Not only that, they're shaped like Taylor Swift's lips with those cute little points on the top of her mouth. Her lower lip is slightly fuller than her top, so it looks pouty.

"Fuck!" I say too loud. I've got to stop thinking about her like that.

"What's wrong now, precious?" she asks, right before taking another bite.

"Nothing." I shove my lunch back into my box, slam the lid shut, and move to another spot away from the vixen, muttering as I go, "Not going there, Ernie. She's not your type." Finding a secluded spot under the only tree on the site, I sit on the ground so I can finish my lunch in peace. Wolfing down what I've got in five minutes, it leaves me a few moments to rest. I lay my head back against the trunk of the tree and shut my eyes. When I do, the only thing I can see is fucking Kennedy Corcoran.

I must have dozed off because when I wake up, J.C. is standing over me with a smirk on his face. "Already dreaming about her, huh?"

"What? No! What're you talking about, old man?"

"You talk in your sleep, Cherry."

"I do not!"

"Yeah, you do," shouts David from behind J.C. He's walking away from my spot on the ground, so I can't be sure he actually heard me.

"Whatever. I wasn't dreaming about anyone."

"Uh-huh," chides J.C. "So, when you whimpered, 'Please, Kenny—"

"Enough!" I shout a little too loud. I lower my voice so only J.C. can hear. "Please. Enough."

"You got it bad, son," he says as he walks away.

"I do not," I mutter. *I don't.* I close my eyes again and concentrate on my breathing. When I open them, she's there. "What now?"

Kenny's hands are on her full hips, which causes her work shirt to gape open around her tits that are almost at my eye level. I catch a glimpse of what lies beneath, and I groan. Her fucking bra is pink too. I adjust my cooler that's on my lap. I refuse to let her see what she does to my dick.

"You need to hurry your ass up and get back to work," she says, tapping her little work boot on the ground. "They're waiting for you to haul in the new delivery."

"Fine! Wait? What? I thought I was digging."

"You've been promoted. You're now hauling deliveries from the trucks to the crew. Congrats. Now get off your ass and get to work." I stare as she turns and walks quickly around the building, her round little bottom wiggling from left to right as she goes.

J.C. cackles from behind me, so I turn and glare at him. "You've got it bad, son."

"Fuck off, J.C.," I grumble, ignoring the nagging thoughts in my head. I find the truck from the lumberyard and get to work. "I'll work all of this sexual tension bullshit right out of my system."

5

# ERNIE FLYNN NEEDS AN ATTITUDE ADJUSTMENT

KENNEDY

Two weeks, that's how long he's worked for me. Two weeks is also the same amount of time I've wanted to strangle Ernie Flynn. The guy is a nuisance. He's cocky, arrogant, and he needs to stop wearing those tight-ass T-shirts. He also needs to invest in some work pants that don't hug his ass and thighs like that. It's dangerous. He could injure himself if he, uh, if his clothes caught on fire or something. Yeah, fire.

*What the hell? We don't have fire here.*

Well, aside from all of that, the guy needs a fucking attitude adjustment. I thought, after letting the whiny pussy move from digging to hauling, his attitude would improve. Instead, he's even surlier than the day he started shoveling. He seems to get along with the others in the crew. He's got a hard-on for me, I guess. I'm tempted to call Donal to get him out of my hair, but he hasn't actually done anything to warrant that. He's been on time, and he works hard—harder than I thought was possible from a cubicle guy like him. So, there's no rationale for firing him. Maybe I can tell Donal his son is distracting me. Yeah, that could work. But then I'd have to explain what I mean by "distracting." Then I'd have to talk about tight shirts and snug pants.

*Welp!* That idea is definitely out. I'll keep working on it. I'm sure I'll think of something.

My thoughts are interrupted by one of my leads, Dillon. "Kenny?"

"Yeah?" *What's wrong now?*

"We're going out tonight. You should meet up Murphy's."

"Can't. My brother's in town. Family's all going to dinner."

"Carter?"

"Yeah. Giants have a week off before the regular season starts up."

"Come after. Bring Carter with ya. I'd love to meet him."

"Maybe. We'll see." The truth is, I could use a beer with my crew because bonding's key to a well-oiled construction machine. I can't cross the line and get too chummy, though. I'm still the boss. I turn to Dillon. "I'll try."

"Sounds good, boss."

## KENNY IN A DRESS IS KILLING ME

### ERNIE

*TFIF.* Thank fuck it's Friday. I toss my cooler over with everyone else's and get to work. At eight in the morning, I'm dead tired. I got no sleep last night. I take that back; I got some sleep—it was rifled with dreams of spankings and handcuffs.

*I need to work her out of my system.* "Maybe I should go out and find someone to fuck tonight," I murmur to myself. It's been a while—a very, long while. Satisfied with that plan, I concentrate on hard work the rest of the day, only getting little glimpses of my she-devil. *My* she-devil? Oh, hell no. Yep, I definitely need to get laid tonight. Definitely.

As I'm loading my gear into my trunk at the end of the day, one of my buddies here on the site slaps me on the back. "Hey, Dave."

"Come out with us tonight. Meet us at Murphy's at eight."

Okay. See? I can have a beer with the guys and find someone to fuck. "Works for me. See you there."

Murphy's is where the guys always go. It's an old Irish bar that's been popular with the blue-collar crowd for years. It's one of my dad's favorite places to go, so I've been there a few times.

After running home to shower and change, I walk in the door and look for Dave. I spy him at a long table surrounded by some of the other guys. J.C. is there along with Cherry #1. "Cherry!" they all shout. Cherry #1 is actually no longer called Cherry. I am. He's now Tim, because, well, that's his name. I can't wait until they hire a new cherry. Then, I can be Ernie again.

"What's up, fuckers?" I say with a laugh.

"Next round is on you, Cherry," someone shouts.

"Damn it." *Of course, it is.*

I head up to the bar, pulling out my wallet at the same time. Leaning against the bar, I check out the place as I wait for my turn to order. It's been a long time since I've been to Murphy's. Funny, it hasn't changed a bit. From the corner of my eye, I spot something red. *That* hair. I turn my head in time to see Kenny walk in, but she's not alone. Next to her is a huge fucker with dark reddish hair and muscles bigger than Hank Flynn's.

"Fuck," I mutter.

I feel the slap, and then, "Uh-oh. Competition," J.C. singsong as he walks back to the table.

Who is she with? And what's she wearing? A fucking dress? She's showing way too much... too much everything. It's a dark color, maybe dark green, and way too low cut and tight around her middle, and the fucking thing barely reaches her knees. Damn, she's got great legs for a f—short chick.

I look down at her feet and see she's wearing some sexy-ass heels too. But the best part is her hair. The flaming mass is all down and curling and swirling around her. It's long. Damn, when she turns, I can see it's almost to her ass. Oh, fuck, her ass. It's nice and round and perky. I can picture her telling me—no, commanding me to fuck her from behind while I spank that sweet thing. I can picture it jiggling under my hand right this minute. My dick starts to awaken, and I groan in disgust. "Not now," I mutter.

"What's the matter?" asks Dave as he sidles up next to me.

"Nothing."

"You've got it bad for her. Everyone knows it. Hell, I'm pretty sure *she* knows it."

"I do not!" I protest a little too loudly. "Who's that guy? He looks like a tool," I mutter.

"Carter."

"Am I supposed to know him?" I look at Dave angrily.

"Carter Corcoran?" He waits for me to recognize the tool's name.

"The football player? From the Giants?"

"Yep, her little brother."

"*Little* brother?" I ask, sounding completely dumbfounded.

"Yeah, thought you knew."

I smile and shake my head. "Nope. But thanks for telling me." Thinking about my woman with another guy was making my head spin. Fuck! *My* woman? I lay my head back and squeeze my eyes shut. This is *not* happening. "This cannot be happening."

"What can't be happening? You've actually got friends?"

My head falls forward, and I look down into a pair of amber eyes. Fucking Kenny Corcoran. "What's up, sweet cheeks?" Yeah, not the best thing to say to my boss, but hell, we're off the clock.

Her tinkling little giggle is sweet. "Oh, Ernest. For that, I'm going to kick your ass on Monday."

I lean in close until my mouth is right next to her ear. "What else do you want to do to my ass? Because I've got a few ideas about what I'd like to do to your sweet ass."

I watch as the dark center of her eyes grow larger and the golden irises sparkle. Whispering in a husky voice, she says, "You have no idea what to do with an ass as sweet as mine. It's out of your league."

I start to respond, but she's gone. She's already back at the table with the other guys. Shit. I'm going to get canned for that, but I couldn't help myself. She smelled *so damn good*—sweet and musky.

With my order in, I head back to the table. The guys are fun. They all laugh easily, and they genuinely like each other. Hell, they even like me. We toast to the job, to Declan, and my dad, and we even toast Kenny. It's then I find out she's got a degree in structural engineering. Not surprising. She knows her shit. What *was* a surprise was finding out she's been working construction since she was fifteen. Her parents had a company, but when they retired, she came to work for Flynn's.

Throughout the night, I've kept an eye on little Kenny. Several guys from the bar, not from work, offer to buy her drinks. I watch one guy try to slide a sneaky palm against her ass, but she pinches his arm so hard I'm pretty sure he was going to cry. Chuckling at that sight, I excuse myself to drain the snake.

When I exit the restroom and start down the hallway, someone tugs on the back of my T-shirt. It's a strong someone. I'm pulled into some sort of storage room. When the door slams behind me, I feel little hands slide up inside my T-shirt.

"You've got ten minutes to make me come, and then I'm out of here."

"Kenny?"

"Who the fuck else would it be?"

Oh, well, there's the waitress who keeps looking at me like I'm lunch and also the bartender, but I don't swing that way. "You practically, uh, spit on me when I, um, hit on you." I'm having a hard time concentrating because now she's using her little, callused palm to stroke my dick from the outside of my pants.

"You gonna get to work, or do I need to find someone else?"

She doesn't have to ask me twice. I pull off my tee and start to unzip my pants, but she shakes her little finger at me. "Oh, no. This test is for you, big guy. Can you make me come in ten minutes?"

I reach for the little tie on her dress. "Fuck yes, I can." I get it untied, and the entire thing opens up. I quickly pull it open the rest of the way and groan. Black. She's wearing a lacy black bra that can barely contain her tits. I look down at her round tummy and keep going. Matching lacy boy short panties. "Fuck, you're hot as sin, woman."

"I know." She leans back against the door. "Get busy."

Oh, there it is. Bossy Kenny, like in my fucking fantasy. I drop to my knees, pulling her panties right along with me. *Shit.* She shaves. I tap the inside of her knees to get her to open them.

"Ask nicely," she purrs in a sexy, deep voice.

"Please open your legs. Let me see."

"See what?" she says, acting coy.

"That pussy. That sweet little pussy."

Sighing, she slowly moves her legs apart. "I suppose."

I dive in headfirst. I promised myself that I wouldn't go down on a woman again after getting that throat STD one time, but this is something I can't pass up. I lick her slit, getting as far back as I can with my tongue. Using my hands to open her up again, I feel her wetness leak down onto my fingers.

"You're so fucking wet for me." When I lick her clit, she moans. "You taste so good, baby."

"Do it again. Faster." Kennedy takes hold of my hair and pushes me into her. "Now!"

Oh, fuck. I think I'm going to come in my damn pants from her bossiness. Her confidence is the sexiest fucking thing I've ever experienced. I pull her to me, clutching her ass with both hands. I slide lower to the ground so I can get in there and push my fingers into her. As soon as I do it, I come in my damn pants. "You're so tight. I can't wait to sink my cock in there."

"Don't plan on that *ever* happening," she says, breathing hard.

I pull away from her. "What? Why not?"

"Only good boys get to use their big cocks on me."

Oh fuck! Everything that comes out of this woman's mouth makes my dick hard. "I'm a good boy."

She makes a tsking sound, and I find myself trying to prove it to her. *I am a good boy, damn it.* I'll show her. In less than ten minutes, she's coming like a porn star. Her juices are sliding all over my hands and face. I look up at her, smiling like a fucking pussy. "Good?"

She stands up, tying her dress back up. "It was fine. You can keep the panties. Your reward."

I reach down and grab them from the floor and shove them into my pocket. She turns and reaches for the doorknob. "If you say one fucking word about this to anyone, I'll spank that ass of yours until it's red."

Oh, fuck. I came. What the hell is wrong with me? Thinking about getting spanked turns me the fuck on. "I won't. I promise."

"Tomorrow night. My place. If you're good...."

"I'll be good."

"I'll call you tomorrow at noon. Answer my call before the third ring."

"I will. I promise." At this point, I think I'd do just about anything to get my dick wet inside Kennedy Corcoran. *Anything.*

# IT'S OFFICIAL. I'M FUCKING WHIPPED

ERNIE

At exactly eleven fifty in the morning, I sit on my couch and hold my phone in my hand. All morning I tried to talk myself out of answering her call, but something deep inside tells me I need to see this through. As soon as I fuck her, I'll be done, so I need to play her game for today. So, yeah, here I sit. At 11:57 a.m., my phone rings. I jump in my seat and stare at the number. It's Dad. I answer the phone in a panic. "What?"

"Jesus, learn to answer the fucking phone like a grown-up, Ernie."

"Sorry, Dad. I'm waiting on an important call. Is anyone sick? Dead? Bleeding?"

"No, I—"

"Then, I'll call you back." I hang up the phone and wait. And wait. Fucking noon rolls by and nothing. No damn call. 12:01 p.m., nothing. At three after twelve, I'm about to toss my cell at the wall; then it rings. I don't recognize the number. It's *her*. I clear my throat and ignore the hard-on that's threatening to implode. I need to sound cool. Hitting the green button, I say, "Hello?" Perfect. I sound cool and manly.

"Ernest?" she says in a soft, sexy voice.

"Yeah?"

"Be at my place at seven tonight. I'll send you my address. Don't be late and don't come empty-handed." She pauses and then adds, "Oh, and, Ernest?"

"Yeah?"

"Don't you dare touch yourself today. That cock of yours is mine tonight."

"Oh, God," I groan into the phone.

I hear her giggle on the other end, then click. Fuck! I need to rub one out now. And what the fuck does "Don't come empty-handed" mean?

I quickly call Claire. "Hello?" she says, sounding sleepy. I ignore the fact I probably work her up. This is important.

"What does 'Don't come empty-handed' mean?"

"Huh?"

"Jesus, Claire. Help me out. When a woman tells you to come to her place and don't come empty handed, What. Does. She. Mean?"

"Well, it could mean that you're supposed to bring flowers or candy. Maybe dinner. Did she say anything else?"

"Nope. Just that."

"Hmm, that's a tricky one. It sounds like you want to impress this girl."

"Maybe."

"Okay, then flowers. No! Candy. Oh, hell, I don't know. Want me to ask Ethan?"

"Fuck no! And don't say a damn word to anyone about this call."

"Got it. Let me know what she meant."

I don't even respond before I hit End. I run my fingers through my hair. I need a haircut. And maybe a new shirt. Jeans? Yeah, I need some new jeans too. I jump off the couch and grab my wallet. I've got enough time to take care of all these details. The added bonus? It'll keep my mind off my dick and Kennedy Corcoran. Well, it'll help anyway.

At 6:55 p.m., I'm standing outside a beautiful arts and crafts bungalow that Chicago is known for. This one looks like it's been lovingly restored, at least from the outside. I check my phone repeatedly until it reads 6:59 p.m. I press the bell so I'm not late. When no one answers, I hit it again.

I'm looking at my feet when I see the door slowly open. My head moves upward as soon as I see two tiny bare feet. Her toes are painted hot pink. They're adorable. I let my eyes move up her bare legs, above her knees, to the edge of sheer black fabric. I suck in a lungful of air as my eyes move up further. She's wearing a robe, if you can call it that. It's practically see-through. And what I see is nothing but skin. I let my gaze move from her bare pussy to her tits. "Holy fuck, Kennedy." Tits for days. They're so big, and somehow, they're still perky. Her dusky nipples are peaked and jutting out from the barely-there fabric. I want to lunge for them and lick and bite them, but I can't do anything until she gives me the all clear.

Moving up to her face, I can tell she's aroused. Her eyes are hooded, seductive and smoky. Her lips, damn, her lips are so beautiful—full and round with cute little peaks at the top. They're painted red to match that flaming hair all around her.

"You finished looking?" She opens the door the rest of the way.

*No.* She turns and walks into a large open-plan living and dining room. The sway of her bare ass under that robe is hypno-tizing. She walks to her sofa and sits down, bringing her legs up beneath her. I shut her front door and follow her.

When I'm standing in front of her, about five feet away, she looks at my hands. "What's all that?"

I'm holding a pile of shit. "Flowers, candy, pizza, beer, wine, and soda. You told me not to come empty-handed."

She throws her head back and laughs. It's a rich, sexy laugh.

I don't get the feeling she's laughing at me so, I add, "I wasn't sure what you meant. So, I went with it."

"Oh, Ernest. You're precious. I meant condoms, but that's fine. I've got those. You can set all of that on the table over there." She points to a dark wood dining table. "Then please walk back this way, slowly."

Oh, heavenly fuck, it's starting. I do as she asks. I set my gifts on the table and walk toward her. "Slower." When I get back to my spot, I stop. "I'd like to see what I'm working with here, Ernest. Please remove your clothing."

I pull off my new polo shirt so fast I get caught up in the three buttons on the front of the shirt. My pants are unbuttoned and unzipped next. I kick off my shoes and slide everything down over my feet. Hopping on one foot, I pull off my left sock and then repeat it on the right foot. When I'm naked, I stand in the same spot. My dick is painfully erect. It's been like that all day.

"Did you do as I asked, Ernie? Did you touch yourself?"

I shake my head. "No."

"That's a very good boy. You look like you could use some relief." I nod fast and furiously. She sighs. "Very well. Walk to me. Slowly."

As slowly as I can, I walk toward her. She moves her feet from the couch to the ground and scoots her body to the edge of the seat. Oh, fuck. This is gonna be good. When I'm directly in front of her, my dick is pointing at her face. She looks up at me with those golden eyes and smirks. Her tongue slips out of her mouth, just the tip, and I watch as it slowly licks the precum that's seeping out of me.

"Mm, Ernie. Yum," she moans.

"Oh, fuck, Kennedy."

She looks up at me and scolds, "No talking."

I nod and shut the fuck up. I bend my head down, holding my breath. When Kennedy's red lips surround the head of my cock, I have to make fists in both hands, so I don't grab her hair, hard. She sucks on the tip of my dick then pulls back, licking under the head. She's so fucking thorough.

"You like it, baby?" she coos softly.

"Fuck yeah." She called me baby, and I loved it. I don't think anyone has ever called me that before.

The next thing I know, her mouth is over me, and she's moving down, down, down. I can't believe she can take that much of me. I'm not small. She grasps my right hand and places it on the top of her head. Then she does the same with my left. "Christ, Kennedy." She wants me to fuck her mouth? I run my fingers through her hair and moan from the feel of that. She takes me deeper until I feel the back of her throat. I hold onto her head and pull back until I'm almost all the way out and press back inside. Not too hard or too fast. She moans when I do it a second time, and the vibration makes my balls draw up. Time stands still as she uses her tongue to stroke my cock. "Kennedy, I'm gonna come." She looks up at me, her eyes smiling. I press into her again and erupt in her mouth. "Fucking Christ." Kennedy takes it all. I'm panting so hard I can barely catch my breath. As I slide out of her, she uses her tongue to lick me clean. It's so dirty; I love it.

Smiling, she stands up and walks away from me. Not sure what to do, so I follow her like a puppy through the dining room into a bedroom lit with candles. Kennedy is standing next to her king-size bed that's covered in a white blanket or sheet. I can't tell which because I don't give a fuck. I watch her reach for the flimsy little belt around her waist. Untying it, she lets her robe fall open. She pushes it off her shoulders and onto the floor until it pools around her feet.

Words can't express what I'm seeing. She's big and round

like I thought, but as she stands there running her hands up her hips to her breasts, one thing is clear. Kennedy exudes confidence and sex.

*This woman is a fucking goddess.*

I hesitate to approach her because she's calling the shots, but I risk it. Then she asks, "What would you like to do next, Ernie?"

Wow, that's a loaded question. I've got to come up with an order of events? I scan her body and then look up at her face. "I'd like to kiss you."

I think I surprised her. She smiles and says, "Well, then, kiss me."

Getting close, I reach my hand out and push a stray curl away from her beautiful face. I trace a few of the freckles with my finger then push my hand into her hair. "You take my breath away, Kennedy."

I think I've surprised her again because she says nothing. She gazes into my eyes and blinks. I lean down and press my lips to hers, but barely. Her breath escapes, and I feel it mix with mine. Stepping close enough for our bodies to touch, I use my fingers to pull her hair, forcing her head to fall back. Turning my head to the right, I swipe her bottom lip with my tongue then suck it into my mouth. Letting go, I say, "Your mouth was made for sin, babe."

"Shut up and kiss me, Ernie."

Using my other hand to keep her still, I lean down for a kiss I'll remember for the rest of my life. When she opens her mouth to me and her little pink tongue slides out to meet mine, I'm rock-hard again. This woman can kiss. I'm so into the feel of our mouths together, I almost miss her hand wrapped around my dick, sliding it up and down. I move my body with her.

"You want me, Kennedy?"

"Oh, yeah. I want you." She pushes me onto the bed, and I

fall back on my ass. Kennedy reaches into the nightstand, pulling out a condom. Tearing it open, she slides it onto my cock, gripping me as she goes. I'd love to go bare, but that's not an option, apparently.

After I'm wrapped up, Kennedy crawls past me until she reaches the headboard. Grasping it with her hands, she turns her head to me, making all of that hair slide further down her back. My eyes pan down her back to the place where her waist dips inward then to her pale ass. It's round and full. She looks like one of those pin-up girls in a calendar from the 1940s. It's that sexy. When she wiggles her hips back and forth, I understand what she wants.

I move onto the bed and crawl toward her on my knees. Sliding both hands over the globes of her ass, I move them up to the narrow part of her waist over skin as soft as silk. She arches her back, pushing her tits out as she goes. I move in closer until our bodies meet. My hands slide under her breasts as my fingers caress her nipples. I pinch and pull on them until I hear her moan, "Fuck me. Ernie. Now."

I reach down and place my dick at her entrance and thrust in hard. "Oh, fuck!" we yell simultaneously.

"You're so…." I can't find the words to describe the feeling of being inside of her. It's like nothing I've ever experience so there are no words. I pull out fast and push in faster. Kennedy meets me each time. Together we find a rhythm that's hot, hard, and fast—I practically piston in and out of her. It's *un-fucking-believable*.

When I feel her pulse around me as she starts to come, I concentrate so I can make it through. It's pointless. The minute she starts to squeeze me, I jerk into her. "Jesus, Kennedy. Goddamn."

I'm breathing like I ran a marathon, but I find myself sliding my hands over her back and sides to help soothe her. She's breathing hard too, her knuckles white from clutching the top of the headboard. "Wow, Ernie."

"'Wow's' an understatement." I pull out of her slowly and see my condom-covered dick. For some strange reason, a sense of disappointment comes over me. Not because of the sex, no way. I think it's because, for the first time in my life, adult or otherwise, I want something more with a woman. I want it all. I sit back on my legs, still gripping her hips. "I may never get enough of you, Kennedy."

She stiffens and pulls away from me. Without saying a word, she slides off the bed, bending down for her robe. She walks quickly into another room that I assume is a bathroom. The door slams shut behind her, and I fall onto my back on the bed. "What the hell was that about?"

I stay on the bed, moving my body up, so my head is on one of her fluffy pillows. I'm tempted to pull the covers back and slide in, but I don't want to piss her off. When she comes back out, she's wearing those tight black exercise pant things and a Rolling Stones T-shirt. I hope this doesn't mean we're done.

8

—————————————

# DON'T GET ATTACHED

KENNEDY

In the bathroom, I stare at myself in the mirror and talk to myself. "Shit. What're you thinking, Kennedy? Sleeping with Ernie Flynn? That's the worse fucking idea you've ever had." I wince when I realize he can probably hear me. He can't know I'm second-guessing this mistake, er, decision.

I pull on the clothes I sleep in, yoga pants and an old tee, then run a brush through my sex hair and stare in the mirror one more time. "I'm sure he's gone by now. Guys like him don't stick around." Pulling the door open, I stop in my tracks. He's still here. Ernie Flynn is reclining naked on my bed.

"You okay?" he asks, looking sincerely concerned.

*WTF?* I gather up my courage and put on my dominant mask again. Lifting my chin and forcing a smug expression on my face, I say, "Of course. I assumed you'd already be dressed and ready to go."

"Why would you assume that? I brought pizza, beer, and wine."

"Well, you can take that with you."

"Can't I stay?" he asks quietly. "We could watch some TV. Whatever you want to watch. We can get cozy."

"I don't 'get cozy,'" I say, using air quotes. "I don't do cuddling afterward." I watch him sit up and start to climb out of bed. *Geez, Ernie, put some pants on.*

"Kennedy, there's something here, between us. You know it. I know it."

"I don't know anything of the sort, Ernest."

Walking toward me, he stops right in front of me. "Kennedy, there's something here."

"You going to get dressed or what?"

"I'll get dressed if you agree to share my pizza and beer while we watch something."

"Fine!" I bark. Irritated. "I'd like it on the record that I think this is a bad idea." A *very* bad idea.

"Noted." As he turns to leave the bedroom, he swats my ass. "You hop on the bed, princess. I'll get the food and drinks."

*Princess?* "Fine."

When he returns, he's got the roses, beer, and the pizza in his hands. "Here. These are for you." He sets six red roses on my lap. "Beer?"

"Sure." *Or ten.* I could use ten beers right now.

He opens my bottle of beer and hands it to me. Lifting the pizza box lid, he says, "I wasn't sure what you liked, so I got half cheese, half pepperoni."

"That's fine."

"What's your favorite?"

"Canadian bacon and pineapple."

He nods. "I'll remember that."

*Whatever.* There's no reason for him to remember anything. We won't be doing this again. I grab the remote and turn on the television that hangs on the wall across from my bed. Scanning the channels, I settle on a movie—a Jane Austen period movie. If that doesn't drive him away, nothing will.

We watch television and eat pizza for several minutes

before I realize he's not going to leave. He's not even going to complain about the movie? All guys complain about British regency-era movies—*all of them*. Instead, he slides over to get closer to me. He brings his arm around my shoulders and scoots so close his body heat makes me drowsy.

I can't help it; I let my head fall onto his shoulder and feel his fingers as they play with my hair. Damn it, that's my kryptonite! I love getting my hair played with, and this guy knows how to do it. He's twisting it loosely around his fingers, and then he moves on to a new strand. Perfect. So perfect, I fall asleep right then and there.

---

I WAKE up to the low murmur of the television and sound of gentle snoring. My room is dark. I've got a blanket over me and two big arms wrapped around me, one hand resting on my hip, the other on my ass. Then I remember...

*Ernie Flynn.* Shit!

He's still here? *Why?* Everything I know about Ernie tells me this isn't his usual modus operandi. It's strange. I've known the guy most of my life, having gone to the same elementary, middle, and high school together. We ran in different circles, but I always knew about the Flynn boys. *Every* red-blooded girl within a fifty-mile radius knew about the Flynn boys.

Even though he was shy and withdrawn in school, I couldn't help but notice him. He was always the biggest one in our class until we were juniors; then some of the other guys caught up to him. But, even then, he was big and strong. He didn't play sports. He hung out in the computer labs and with a couple other nerds, but he was mostly alone. I had several classes with him our senior year. I used to sit behind him and watch him. He barely took notes in class—hell, he barely stayed awake—but he always blew everyone else away on tests. He's *that* smart.

So, yeah, I had a little crush on him. He didn't notice me, though. I'm not sure he noticed anyone. He wasn't a monk. I know he hooked up with girls back then. Now, since coming back from college, he's slept with a bunch of people. I know this because word gets around; plus, I know some of the girls. They're friends of mine. The things they said about him weren't exactly flattering. One common complaint all the girls had was Ernie Flynn was an asshole afterward. As soon as they were finished, he kicked them out of his place. He's a loner. He doesn't want a girl in his life, let alone a relationship. I know this for a fact.

*So, why is he still here?*

God, what was I thinking? I've got to get rid of him. When the idea hits me, I smile. It's genius. He's a commitment-phobe. What does a commitment-phobe fear the most? Answer: a stage-five clinger. I giggle softly to myself as I begin to plan.

9

## I'VE GOT IT BAD

ERNIE

When she falls asleep, I grab a throw from the end of the bed and place it on her; I don't want her to get chilled. I snuggle down into the bed. While I hate the movie, I can tell it's one of her favorites because she repeated some of the lines to herself, so I leave it. For just a split second, I wonder who the fuck I am. The old Ernie would have taken the remote out of her hand and changed it to something bloody with bombs and shit. Or better yet, an alien flick. But the second I met this person, something in me clicked. Maybe clicked isn't the right word. Cracked. Something inside me cracked and something good started to ooze out of me. Okay, that all sounds pretty fucking weird and gross, but that's all I've got for now, so you can just deal. Anyway, sleeping against Kennedy is surreal. I've only fallen asleep with two other women, my best friend Hammer and my college girlfriend. I forget her name. With Hammer and me, we'd cozy up on the couch to watch something; she'd fall asleep while I played with her hair, like with Kennedy tonight. The difference? I didn't get hard as granite when Claire Hammer was with me. Well, I did once, but let's not go there.

Lying here with Kennedy in my arms gives me fucking chills. Her soft, lush body is molded to my harder one. I slide my palm down her body. It dips a little at her waist then raises right back out to her full hip. Her skin is smooth and silky. I keep that hand there as I let the other one scrape through her glossy red locks. It ends up on her plump little ass and stays put.

*Why did I ever think she was fat? She's curvy, yes. Voluptuous, absolutely. But fat? Not a chance.*

I fall asleep with my hands full of Kennedy Corcoran, and I've never been happier.

I wake up feeling hands running slowly up and down my chest. They skim first over my right nipple, then my left. Small fingers pinch that nipple, and I flinch at the sensation. Then I feel them move down, down, down, right into my boxers. Her hand wraps around my now hard cock to stroke me. "Kennedy?" My voice sounds rough and gravely.

"Wake up, baby," she coos softly.

"Does my girl need me?"

She stops stroking me for a second but starts again. "Yeah. Your girl needs you, Ernie," she whispers in my ear. She trails kisses from the side of my face to my mouth. Squeezing my dick, she whispers in a husky voice, "Who does this dick belong to, Ernie?"

Oh, fuck. She's claiming me. "You. It's yours, Kennedy." Forever if she wants it.

"Fucking right it is." She squeezes me a little too hard, but I say nothing because she might stop if I fuss. "If you're a good boy, I'll let you have more of my sweet pussy. You want that?"

"Yes," I say, choking a little bit "Yeah, I want that. I'll be good." I want to say more, but I only think about the fact that I'll never fuck anyone but Kennedy. I'll never want to.

"Slide those boxers off. Let me show you what I want you to do."

"Okay." Oh, fuck. This woman is gonna be the death of me, but I'll die happy.

10

——————

## PLAN A

KENNEDY

*Fuck!* I thought for sure when I asked him *"Who does this dick belong to, Ernie?"* that he'd jump out of bed and run for the hills. No commitment-phobe I've ever heard of would have answered, *"You. It's yours, Kennedy."*

*Ugh, now what?*

I watch him slide his boxers down his legs and kick them off somewhere into the darkened bedroom. Sighing, I realize I've got to do it. I've got to pull the fucking trigger. I slide off the bed and undress. There's enough light coming in the window from the streetlight for him to see me. He's watching me.

Taking a slow breath in then out, I prepare myself. Whenever I've tried this in the past, it's ended badly. Guys don't react well when a larger woman wants to be on top. They may *think* they want it, but by the time I'm sitting astride them, they panic like I'm going to smother them or some shit. Ernie Flynn will be no different. Hell, he might even be worse. He may throw me off onto the ground as he runs out the door.

It's going to be embarrassing *for me*, something I don't usually go for. I avoid feeling embarrassed or even bad about myself whenever I can. I grew up with three brothers who spent a good deal of time teasing me. I was the second kid. My brother Johnson is the oldest; I'm second, then Carter, and the youngest is Clinton. Yeah, my parents have a thing for political names.

Anyway, for years they teased me relentlessly about my hair, my height, and my weight. That is until they didn't. I'm not sure what happened or when it happened exactly, but one day when I was about sixteen, it stopped. They were suddenly nice to me—almost sweet. It bothered me at first, but then I kind of liked it. They continued to tease each other. They still do. But me? They leave me alone. Shaking off the thoughts of my brothers—'cuz that can ruin perfectly good sex—I look over at Ernie. He's still sitting on the bed waiting. For instructions? "Lay down in the center of the bed on your back."

He quickly scoots into the center and lays back. Without another word, I put my knee on the bed and then the other. I'm now above him, looking down at him. His hands are next to his body, twitching. He wants to touch me, but not yet. I use my palm to explore his body. If this is going to be the last time I get to play with Ernie Flynn, I want to make it last.

I notice his pectorals are well developed. His nipples are hard and flat. I lean over and swipe my tongue over the one closest to me, causing him to moan. "Shhh, quiet." I slide my fingers back and forth over the other nipple while I take my time licking and nibbling on the one closest to me. He's staying quiet, but his body is writhing on the bed. I peek down at his dick, and it's twitching too. "You're very responsive, Ernest."

"Uh-huh," he pants.

"Are you ready for me, baby?" I ask in my sweetest voice.

"Fuck! Kennedy. Yesss," he hisses.

I reach into my nightstand and pull out a condom. Tearing open the package, I slowly roll the condom over him, using a little pressure as I go. He moans loudly, but I don't shush him this time. "You're such a good boy, Ernie."

"I am?"

He loves the praise, and it turns me on too. "Yes, you're a very good boy." I love being dominant in bed. Not all the time, but right now, hell yes. Hearing Ernie Flynn submit to me makes me so wet—and a little sad. Sad this has to end. Because, in five minutes, it'll be over. "Move your legs together." He slides them closed and waits. Scooting closer to him, I place my hands on his chest as I lift my right leg up and over him to the other side of his thigh.

I look down at him. He's watching me closely, but he hasn't said a word. On my knees, I slide up over his cock. Using my hand, I pull him up until the head of his dick is at my entrance. I look down and find him staring at the place where we're about to join. Shrugging, I go for it. I press him to me and slowly sit down.

"Oh fuck," he moans. "You've got the tightest fucking pussy, Kennedy."

"I know. It's sweet, isn't it?" I can't believe he hasn't thrown in the towel. He will after I make my next move.

"It's the sweetest fucking pussy in the world."

With my hands on his stomach, I push back up. Above him again, I plop back down. Hard.

He grunts then moans. "Do that again. Jesus. Faster," he pants.

I'll be damned. His hands move around my thick waist to help me move up, and then he yanks me back down. "Faster, baby. Please," he begs.

Up and down, we work in sync. My breasts are bouncing so much I should feel self-conscious, but Ernie's muttering sexy things as he watches them. "You're so fucking hot, Kennedy. Jesus, where've you been all my life?"

I don't answer. I'm still not close to an orgasm, and it's frustrating me. Somehow, Ernie knows. "Babe, let me." He sits up, wrapping his arms around me. Kissing me sweetly, he moves me to my back all while he's still inside me. "Spread your legs wide, princess."

I do as he commanded and feel him slide out, then thrust in so hard I gasp. He pumps into me several times, and then his fingers find my clit, circling and pinching while he moves into me. "Oh, God. I'm close, Ernie. Don't stop."

"Never," he grunts. "Never. Come for me. Come."

I come so hard I see stars floating around Ernie's head. He comes moments later and then falls down on top of me. "Kennedy," he whispers as he wraps his arms around me. "Sleep, baby."

Well fuck, so much for plan A. On to plan B. I feel a blanket thrown over me, and I'm out like a light.

# MEETING THE FAMILY

## ERNIE

I wake up with a beautiful woman wrapped around me. I must have rolled over to my side in the night because I'm facing away from her. I turn my head back so I can see her. Tendrils of her hair are everywhere—on my arm, across my face, and spread all around her like flames. She's got her tits pressed against my back and one short little leg thrown over my hip while the sheets and blankets are all pushed to the end of the bed. I smile. I'm not sure which part of last night or this morning is making me smile, maybe it's all of it. I slip out from beneath her leg as carefully as I can. I need to piss, but I don't want to wake her. She looks like a fucking angel when she sleeps. Grabbing the sheet and blankets, I carefully cover her up, so she doesn't get cold. In that instant, I remember the night me and Claire.... God, I was such an asshole. That night, I got up from the couch we were both sleeping on, and as I went, I took the blanket with me. The one and only blanket from the sofa. Hell, I didn't even need it, but I still took it, leaving my best friend naked and completely uncovered—without a goddamn blanket. "Fuck," I mumble to myself. I was such a dick. I look back down at Kennedy and blink. What happened? *What is it about this girl that makes me look at her differently than anyone else?*

On my way to the john, I spy my boxers and my polo shirt that was abandoned early on. I snatch them up before slipping into her bathroom to take care of business. I search her cupboards and find a new toothbrush in its packaging. I open it up and brush my chompers. I find a cloth and wash my face and other parts, then borrow her brush and run it through my new short hair. Damn, she didn't even notice the haircut. Well, she did have other things on her mind, I guess. I smirk at myself in the mirror. "Damn, what a night."

Stepping out of her bathroom, I make my way to the living room. I find my pants and socks on the floor where I left them. Remembering the blowjob, I stop dead in my tracks. Fuck! That was, hands down, the best hummer I've ever gotten. I start to get hard thinking about those plump lips wrapped around me.

*Better not get too excited. She's tired. I don't want to piss her off first thing in the morning.* I slip my jeans on, then my socks. I ignore my shoes because I'm not ready to leave. I won't walk out on her and make her wonder why I left without kissing her goodbye. *Holy fuck. When did I turn into my pussy brother, Ethan?* Answer? The day I saw Kennedy Corcoran. I make my way into her kitchen and gape at the place. I can tell the room has been completely redone, but it's all finished to look like its original to the home. Well, except for the top-of-the-line stainless appliances. The counters are marble while the backsplash is made of glass subway tiles in shades of blues and greens. I pull open a cupboard door and marvel at how neat everything is with the plates in one cupboard, glasses in another. Hammer tried to get me to organize like that, but I never wanted to do it. Now, I can see the benefit.

As I search for coffee and filters, I hear the front door open.

I step out of the kitchen in time to see three huge dudes and an older couple, around my dad's age, walk into the living room. The woman looks like an older version of Kennedy. Must be her parents. And those must be her brothers because I recognize Carter from the bar the other night.

I make my presence known by clearing my throat and saying, "Hey." Weak. I know.

"Oh, hello!" says the mom in a high-pitched squeak. "Oh dear, we didn't mean to interrupt, uh, anything."

"You're not. Kennedy's still asleep. Do you want me to wake her?"

"Oh, heavens no. She'll smell the breakfast casserole, and that'll wake her. Works every time."

I nod, preparing to reply when one of the big guys asks, "Who the fuck are you?"

"Clinton Corcoran, you watch your mouth!" says the mom.

"Sorry, Mom." Turning from her back to me, he repeats, "Seriously, who the hell are you?"

"I'm Kennedy's boyfriend."

"Her what?" shouts Carter.

"No way!" says the third brother. "She'd have told us if she had a guy."

"We're new."

Clinton scoffs and then glares at me. "How new?"

"Is that any of your business?" I spit.

"Yeah!" he says, stomping toward me.

"Boys!" shouts the father. "Enough! We'll let Kennedy explain. Leave the poor boy alone."

"Whatever," grunts the third one, –who shall remain nameless.

The douchebag brothers all walk back into the living room and find places to sit or stand.

"Well, let me put this in the oven to warm. Is there coffee?" asks the mom.

"I was making coffee." I follow her into the kitchen. Wow, I had no idea it'd be *Meet the Family* day at Kennedy's. Honestly, I'm not sure I'm ready for this shit.

12

---

# MY STUPID, OVERPROTECTIVE BROTHERS

KENNEDY

I wake up alone and warm, covered in seven layers of blankets. Thankfully, there's no sign of the giant nerd that shared my bed last night. I let out a sigh of relief. "He's gone." Don't get me wrong, Ernie's a great guy. Fantastic in bed, that's for sure. A lot better than I gave him credit for after hearing tales of his exploits from my friends. They said things like, "He's fucking selfish." And "I didn't even get off," said my high school friend, April. "He's tiny," claimed another college friend. I snort at that lie. He's definitely *not* tiny.

I roll onto my back, kicking off the blankets as I go. When I sit up, stretching my arms up above my head, I realize I'm sore. Good sex equals sore body parts. I slip out of bed in search of my tee and yoga pants. As I'm bent in half, ass in the air, I hear him. "Babe?"

I squeak, standing up quickly, so much so I nearly fall back onto the bed. I pull the T-shirt up to cover myself. "Wh-what are you still doing here?"

"Making coffee. How do you take yours?"

What the ever-loving fuck? "Uh, just cream. Then we need to—"

I don't get another word out when I hear my mother's voice. "Kennedy? You finally up, sleepyhead?"

What the ever-loving fuck? I stare at Ernie. "My parents are here?" I whisper-hiss.

"And your brothers. Uh, I don't think they like me very much. I'm pretty sure the young one wants to beat the shit out of me."

"Me too," I mutter under my breath.

"What's that?"

"Nothing. I'll be out in a second."

"Your mom put the casserole in the oven. Breakfast will be ready shortly, so don't dawdle," Ernie deadpans. He meant it.

*Don't dawdle?* What the ever-loving fuck?

I dawdle. I spend as much time in my bathroom as I possibly can. Then, the knock on the door reminds me I can't hide forever. "What?"

"Sweetie?" says my mom through the door. "Breakfast is almost ready."

"Okay. Out in a jiffy," I say with clenched teeth. There was no warning to this impromptu little breakfast. My folks have strict instructions not to show up at my house unannounced. It's not that I don't want them here; I just want to know when they're all going to descend upon me since I'm usually braless and in sweats. I keep my house pretty clean but not "Mom clean," if you know what I mean. Forewarned is forearmed, as they say.

I open the door to see an older version of myself staring back at me. "Hey, Mom." Kissing her cheek and giving her a hug, I whisper in her ear, "You should have warned me."

"Oh, I know, honey, but Carter has to leave soon, and he wanted to see you before he left for New Jersey. So, we thought... breakfast!" she says "breakfast" with a whole lot of perky. It's too much pep this early in the morning.

"Fine," I say, slumping my shoulders. "Let's go face the firing squad."

"About that. I didn't realize you had a boyfriend."

"I don't."

"Well, he said he was your boyfriend."

"He's not."

"Why not? He's very handsome, honey. Isn't that one of Donal Flynn's boys?"

"Yeah."

"He's a catch, honey."

"Mom?" I turn to face her. "He's not my boyfriend. I don't do boyfriends." *Anymore.*

"Not in the past, but maybe—"

I run my hand over my forehead. "Mom? Can we talk about this later? I have a fire to put out. That is if they haven't taken him out back and beaten him bloody already."

"Right. Good idea, sweetie. Let's go."

When I get to my dining room slash living room, I stop dead in my tracks. Ernie's holding a pot of coffee out, refilling my dad's cup. Dad's smiling at Ernie and chatting happily; Carter is leaning on the wall next to the front window staring daggers at Ernie. Johnson is sitting in my side chair, gripping his cup with both hands while watching Ernie like he knows exactly where to bury the body, and Clinton? Well, he's sitting at my dining table eating some of the leftover pizza. He's also staring at Ernie's back, no doubt plotting his demise.

So, I may have mentioned that my brothers stopped making fun of me at about age sixteen. What I neglected to mention was that they stopped doing that and started "protecting" me. I put that word in quotes because it wasn't so much protecting me as it was beating the ever-loving shit out of any guy that talked to me or talked *about* me. It was problematic, to say the least. They, essentially, frighten off any potential suitors until I went off to college—or at least that was the goal when I chose to go to school far, far away from my brothers. I thought distance meant they wouldn't be able to scare guys away. Until they did. Case in point, Carter came to visit me in college, and for some reason, my then "friend" James broke up with me immediately after that weekend. The bastard. I found out weeks later that Carter had James by the neck against the concrete wall of my dormitory. It was his warning to "stay the fuck away from my sister" and to "spread the word." Needless to say, college was lonely as hell.

So, yeah, the scene before me has played out before. I doubt even Ernie Flynn will stick around after my brothers threaten him with his life. No guy has ever stuck around. Actually, I should have thought of this. It could have been plan C if plan B hadn't worked. But I don't have to worry about plan B anymore. This is going to be it for Ernie and me.

13

---

## JUDGMENT DAY

ERNIE

While Kennedy and her mom, Jo, work in the kitchen, I'm stuck in the living room with her dad, Herb, and the three guerrillas she calls brothers. While I sit on the couch next to Herb, he chitchats about retirement, the construction business, and sports. I'm only paying partial attention because Clinton, Carter, and Johnson are all glaring me at. It's then I realize they're all named after former presidents.

"So, why the presidents?" I turn to ask Herb.

"What, son?"

"The kids. Why'd you name them after presidents?"

Herb rolls his eyes. "Their mother wanted those names. After the hard time she had giving birth to each one of those monsters," he says, pointing to the boys, "I let her name them whatever the hell she wanted."

I guess that's a good enough answer. Maybe I'll ask Kennedy about that. "I sure hope Kennedy doesn't want to name our kids after presidents. I don't like themes."

Herb turns to face me. He's smiling, sort of. When I hear someone growl, my eyes move over to Carter then they slide over to Johnson. They're both leaning forward in their seats like they want to jump me. What the hell did I just say?

"You're not going to have any balls to impregnate our sister, asshole," mutters Clinton.

"Because we're going to rip them from your pussy body," adds Johnson.

"Boys. Now, come on...," mutters Herb.

That's it? That's all Herb's going to say to them? They're practically threatening me. I'm about to give my rebuttal when Jo pokes her head out of the kitchen. "Herb, honey, I forgot orange juice. Would you quickly run to the corner market and get some? Breakfast will be ready in ten minutes."

"Sure thing, Jo Jo." Herb stands and reaches back to make sure he's got his wallet. I turn to watch him stroll through the living room and out the front door.

*Shit.*

"Alone at last," grumbles Carter.

"Sweet. What should we talk about? What big assholes you three are?" I quip.

"Ha, ha. I think we should step out onto the porch for a little chat," suggests Johnson.

"Sure thing, let's go, motherfuckers." I grew up with the Flynns. This macho bullshit is a daily occurrence for me. I can stand my ground. We move through the living room and out the front door. I move to the center of Kennedy's covered front porch. It's as nice as the rest of the house. "So, what do you assholes want to say?"

Clint lunges for me, but Carter holds him back and says, "We don't want to hurt you. We want you to leave."

"Nope." I'm not leaving.

"We want you to stay out of her life," adds Johnson.

"Nope." I shake my head.

"I want to kick your fat ass," says the shortest one. Clinton's got to be six feet two.

"I'm not fat, you little prick."

"Who're you calling little?'

"You, Clinton." I cross my arms over my chest, puffing it out a tad.

That's all it takes for Clinton to lose his shit. He lunges for me, swinging his fist as he goes. I take one big step back and watch him fly past me onto the wood plank porch floor. He grunts when he makes contact.

Carter chuckles at his little brother but stops as soon as he makes eye contact with me. "I can't touch you. They'd suspend me from the team, but, Jesus, I wish I could."

"Too bad." I shrug and turn to the oldest. "Johnson, you want to take a swing at me?"

"Oh, fuck yeah," he says, stomping toward me. I raise my fists, ready for battle. As he pulls his fist back, we hear it—the screech heard round the world.

"What the ever-loving fuck?" screeches Kennedy at the top of her lungs.

We all stop moving to stare at her. Her face is as red as her hair, and pieces of it have fallen out of the bun thing on top of her head, her golden eyes glowing. "Fucking glorious," I mutter.

"What'd you say?" asks Johnson with his fist still poised ready to strike.

"Your sister is fucking glorious when she's pissed. All the time, actually, but when she's pissed, she's on fire," I say with awe.

They all turn to look at her. Carter nods slowly as Johnson lowers his fists. "She is, isn't she?"

"She's a fucking spitfire," I add.

"She sure is," says Clinton as he pulls himself up into a sitting position.

"And she's all mine, assholes. So get used to it."

The three of them turn to me with strange expressions on their faces. Resignation? I sure as hell hope so because I'll fight them all at once if I have to. I just don't want to.

"I belong to no man, asshole," spits Kennedy. "I want you to leave now," she says, pointing at me. She turns to her brothers. "I want you three dumbasses to eat and then leave. Don't you ever come to my house again without calling first, you got me?"

"Yeah," they all grumble at the same time.

"I mean it? And stop trying to beat up every guy I have a fling with. It's getting fucking old."

*Fling?* I know what a fling feels like, and this isn't it. I shrug and walk back into the house. After finding my shoes near the sofa, I slip them on, grab my keys, and walk back out onto the porch. I pull my woman to me. "See you later, princess." I lean down and kiss her. It's deep, and there's a lot of tongue. The brothers groan with disgust, but fuck them. They could've gone into the house. Instead, they decided to watch. "I'll call you."

I'll do more than call her.

I'm gonna marry that girl.

# 14

## PLAYING PRETEND

### KENNEDY

I get to the site early on Monday to get organized. At six in the morning, I unlock my trailer and step inside. Administrative work is a big part of my duties on a site like this. Most of that relates to making sure we've got the appropriate permits, paying invoices, ordering supplies, lining up inspections, submitting payroll to the central office on time, and writing up any employees who can't follow the rules—*Timmy*. It's busy work, but sometimes it's a nice break from dealing with the daily bullshit of working with all that testosterone.

By eight, everyone is on the site and heading to their project areas. We're in a rush to get the exterior of the building to the point that will enable us to work inside when the cold and winter weather hits. It's almost October, so time is of the essence. I'll have to ride these guys harder than usual to keep them on pace.

As I walk around, checking on the various teams, I catch a glimpse of Ernie. He's in the process of unloading sixty-pound bags of mortar mix around to the back of the building. Right now, he's got a bag on each shoulder. When he sees me, he stops in his tracks, and I watch his lips split into a wide smile. "Hey, Kennedy," he says happily.

I feel a smile start to crack onto my face, but a snicker behind me reminds me where I am. I gather myself up, push my shoulders back, and say, "Cherry." I watch his face fall to a frown. Damn, I can't deal with this shit with Ernie right now, so I turn and walk in the opposite direction.

What fucking plan am I on now? There was plan A: attempting to crush him during sex—didn't work. Plan B: becoming a stage-five clinger—still an option, and plan C: letting my brothers scare him off, which didn't work—yet. Maybe I need a plan D.

I march around the entire building, avoiding the path that Ernie's taking as he moves the mortar mix to the masonry guys. "Plan D...." I shake my head as I reach the architect. I need to take my mind off of Ernie and stay far away from him in the process. I don't want to get the poor guy's hopes up. It's not going to work out between Ernie and me. It just isn't.

By Wednesday, I think he's figured out I'm ignoring him. He tried to eat lunch with me Tuesday, but I got up and moved into my trailer, making the excuse I needed to make some calls. Today's Thursday, so I ask Dave to put Ernie on the three inspectors we have coming in today. His job will be to follow them around, making notes of everything they say and do. It's a mindless and unnecessary task, but he'll be out of my sight for the remainder of the day. Or so I thought.

At around three o'clock, the plumbing inspector shows up to approve the plumbing rough-in. All the digging Ernie did as part of his training was so the plumbers could lay pipe. See? Ernie's work wasn't for naught. When the inspector shows up, I realize he's new and that I know him. He's in dark suit pants, a blue dress shirt, and a tie. The other thing I notice is the guy is built like a linebacker and he's still smokin' hot. It's not like three or four years would have made him ugly.

As he approaches, I look up from my stack of invoices and see a sexy smirk slide across his pretty face. "Is that Kenny Corcoran I see before me?"

"Yeah." I pull off my hard hat. "Hey, Brock." My wild rat's nest falls out all around my head. I need a damn haircut.

He extends both of his arms in that universal sign that says, "Hey, let's hug." I oblige. When our bodies meet, I can't help but notice how tightly he wraps me up in his arms. I let go after a couple of seconds, but Brock hangs on. And on. Let me just say he lingers, and I let him.

Looking up from our hug, my eyes travel up his big body to a beautiful dimpled smile. Jesus, dimples are my weakness—yeah, I've got a lot of weaknesses. I smile back because I can't help it. When he speaks, his voice is deep and sexy. "Kenny, how long has it been?"

"A few years," I say, attempting to be nonchalant. Nonchalant about the fact that the hottest guy in my engineering program is right in front of me. Brock Lancaster, the guy with a name that belongs on a soap opera, was the guy every woman and some men wanted to bed in college. The guy I fantasized about on numerous occasions. *That* Brock Lancaster is standing right in front of me.

"Too long. You look—" He pauses. That's not a good thing when someone has to take a second to think of a compliment. "—good, Kennedy."

I let out a stupid giggle like some fucking schoolgirl. "You too, Brock." There's a slight lull in the conversation because I'm a little tongue-tied.

"I'm here to inspect your pipes."

Okay, that was funny. I start to giggle again because the first thing that came to mind was to say, "Oh, you can inspect *my* pipes, Brock Thompson," but of course I don't. Instead I say, "Great, I've been waiting for you."

He moves in a little closer to me and asks softly, "You have?"

I blink up at him and bite my bottom lip, so I don't confess my love of Brock Lancaster—er, I mean plumbers, er, plumbing, "I sure have," I say, fluttering my eyelashes.

He places his big left hand on the side of the building and leans inward until we're only about ten inches apart. His right hand moves up to my face, pushing a strand of my hair away from my eyes. "I'll go get started. I'll let you know if I need you. Sound good?"

"Sounds good."

He turns away from me and starts to walk, but then he turns. "But, Kenny?"

"Yeah," I say, a little too breathlessly for my liking.

"I'm gonna need you."

"Uh"—*Holy fuck*—"right. Yeah. Okay. Let me know," I reply nervously. Jesus, what is it about this guy that makes me act like a teenage girl watching Harry Styles sing? I turn and march over to the water cooler. I need a drink. Gulping down the entire glass with one go, I'm so startled I nearly spit it all out again when Ernie sneaks up on me.

"What the fuck was that?" Ernie snarls.

"What are you talking about?" I casually say as I sip my water.

"That fucker in the suit. You let him touch you?"

I toss the paper cup into the trash and stare up at him. "Ernie, that's none of your concern."

"The fuck it isn't. You think I'm gonna stand by and watch some fucking tool in a suit touch what's mine? You've got another thing—"

"In my office!" I point angrily to my trailer. "Now!"

I've caught him off guard, but he doesn't argue. He turns,

stomps to my trailer, wrenches open the door, and waits for me to enter first. Fuck, he's being all gentlemanly. I stomp up the stairs and walk toward my small desk. Hands on hips, I wait for the door to slam behind him. Once he's inside, I start my rant. "I'm not your fucking property, Ernie!"

"Yes, you—"

I hold my hand up to get him to stop speaking. "That's enough!"

He stops talking and stares at me. I'm sure I look like a raving lunatic with my hair all crazy, my face red, and, according to what Ernie said on my porch last weekend, my eyes are no doubt glowing like a demon's. I take a deep breath and say the words I know he'll respond to. "You're behaving like a very, very bad boy, Ernie."

He must be a little shocked by that statement because his body goes rigid at my words. "No, I'm not."

"You are, and now you're talking back to me."

"I'm not."

"I think it's time you were punished. This attitude of yours has got to stop." Okay, I have no idea where this is coming from, but I'm going with it.

"P-Punished?" he stutters.

"Yep. Unbutton your pants. Pull them down to your thighs."

He slowly unbuttons his pants but says nothing. When he pushes them down, he's aroused, not to his full glory but close. "Walk to my desk and put your hands down on the top."

He follows orders, warily. The desk is low, so he's got to bend at the waist. I know it's wrong, but watching him do this is turning me on. I reach the top of my desk and take my metal drafting ruler in my hand. One side is metal, the other cork. I roll it so the metal side is down. "Now, Ernie, do you agree that you deserve a punishment for the way you spoke to me?" I slap the ruler against my hand. Ouch.

"Y-Yes."

"Good. I'm going to spank you six times, and you're going to count for me. Do you understand?"

"I, uh, yeah."

"Good. Now, if this is too much, use a safe word. Uh, say the word 'butterfly' if it's too much. All right, Ernie?"

"Butterfly. Yeah."

Okay, confession time. I've never in my life spanked anyone, but I've read a million BDSM romance books, so that pretty much makes me an expert. I pull my arm back behind me and bring it forward to his bare ass and *slap!* The ruler hits his bare bottom.

Ernie flinches and mutters a curse, but he only says, "One."

"Good boy, Ernie."

*Slap!* "Two."

I swat him two times quickly. His ass is getting red. I want this to be over soon.

"Three. Four," he says fast.

I tried to be careful, hitting each ass cheek twice and avoiding spots I've already swatted. I do it two more times and listen for him to squeak out, "Five. Six."

"There." I toss the ruler on my desk. "All done. You can pull your pants up now."

I watch him as he stands to full height. I look down and see his dick is at its full length. It looks hard and angry. Precum is seeping out of the top. I look up at his face. There's perspiration on his forehead. "You liked that, Ernest?"

"Yeah."

I look down again. "I don't want you touching yourself tonight. Do you understand me?"

He groans. "Yeah."

"Good. Now get back to work. The plumbing inspector may need your help."

He says nothing as he gingerly steps down from my trailer. I watch him walk away, wincing a little with each step. I feel regret now. That was completely out of line and inappropriate. But, damn, I'm so wet now. Ernie turns me on so fucking much—even more than sexy Brock Lancaster.

An hour passes, and there's been no sign of hot plumber *or* Ernie. I decide to make sure Ernie hasn't killed the guy. Turning the corner of the building, I watch Ernie wincing as he bends to pick something up. Shit. Did I hurt him? "Ernie!" I shout angrily. I'm not angry, though. But the guys don't need to get their nose in my shit.

"Yeah?"

"My office! Now!"

"What the fuck did I do now?" he spits.

"No back talk!"

He shuts up and follows me, slowly, to my trailer. I open it for him this time and watch him struggle to make it up the steps.

Once inside, I demand, "Pull your pants down, Ernie."

"Not again," he whines. "I was good."

"Shut up and pull your pants down." He makes a snuffling noise and unbuttons then unzips his jeans, slowly pulling them down. I watch in horror as his ass comes into full view. The red lines from the ruler are now angry welts. I walk to get a closer look, and my heart melts. "Oh, baby," I coo. "I didn't mean to hurt you."

I touch his bottom gently, and he jumps slightly. I walk around to face him. "Ernie, I'm sorry," I whisper. I'm completely serious and sincere. He looks down at me, several emotions crossing his face. I think I see fear, which I hate, and sadness. But then he gives me a slow smile.

"It was hot, Kennedy. It hurts like a motherfucker now. Maybe next time use your little palm instead of a fucking metal ruler."

"There won't be a next time," I mutter angrily.

"What? Why not?" he says, sounding confused. "I'm.... I liked it."

"We'll see. Right now, I want you to get your things and go home. When you get there, take off your clothes, lay on your bed on your stomach, and I'll be there after work. Leave your door unlocked. Do you understand?"

"You're coming over?"

"I'll be there with something to put on those welts."

"Oh, okay. You know where I live?" he says as he slowly slides his jeans back up.

Shit, that's got to hurt. "Yeah, I've got it in my files."

"Right. Of course. See you later, Kennedy."

# 15

## NURSE KENNEDY

### ERNIE

It takes me forever, but I finally make it up the four flights of stairs to my apartment. Unlocking the door, I step inside, tossing my lunch shit onto the floor near the door. I push the door shut, making sure I leave it unlocked. After getting a glass of water from the kitchen, I head into my bedroom. I strip out of my work clothes and lay down, face-first, on my bed.

"Shit!" I groan. My ass hurts. But, damn, that whole scene in her trailer was hot as fuck. If I hadn't been in pain, I would have tried for a quick fuck in her trailer. But it hurt too much. I pull my arms up and wrap them around my pillow. The cool air of my apartment feels good on my butt.

I guess I dozed off for a while because a cool hand on my back awakes me. "Ernie?"

"Yeah?"

"Let's get you into a cool shower."

"Okay." I stand up and follow Kennedy into my bathroom. I'm already stripped bare, so I watch as she pulls off her work clothes. "What're you doing?"

"I'm going to clean you."

*Fuck, yeah! Stay calm, Ernie.* My dick's getting hard, so I guess she'll figure out how much I like the idea. Stepping into the shower, Kennedy adjusts the temperature. When it's where she wants it, she reaches her hand out for mine. I place it in her little palm and follow her inside. Standing in front of her, I marvel at Kennedy as she works on me. She uses her bare palms to gently wash my butt but uses a cloth to clean the rest of me.

"Bend down. I want to wash your hair." I bend so I'm eye level with her amazing tits. The nipple in front of me is about to poke me in the eye. Okay, I can't help myself; I stick my tongue out and swipe it across her hard nipple.

"Ernie, not now."

"Fine," I grumble.

"I'm here to take care of you. You need to let me."

*She's here to take care of me?* I fucking love the sound of that. "Okay."

After our shower, she treats my welts with witch hazel. It's supposed to make the swelling go down.

"We'll put some ice on it as soon as I've got you tucked back into bed."

I dress in loose boxers and a clean tee. I also pull out one of my T-shirts for her to wear. It's snug on her in all the right places while falling all the way down to her knees. It looks perfect.

"I brought dinner. Are you hungry?"

"Starving. What'd you bring?" I don't care what it is. I'll eat it.

"I picked up a few things. I'll make you a plate and bring it into your room. Now, go lie down."

I follow orders, lying on my stomach. Moments later, she's back in my room with a plate heaping with food. She places a hand towel on my sheet and sets the plate on that. Utensils and a napkin are next. "What would you like to drink? I brought milk and juice, but I see you've got soda and beer in your fridge."

"Milk sounds good. Thank you, Kennedy."

She gives me a small smile and leaves again. I look down at my plate, and my stomach growls. There's crispy chicken strips, gooey macaroni and cheese, and green beans. "Comfort food." *Awesome.*

I push myself up to sit on my ass, but when I feel the bed beneath me, I wince in pain. Quickly, I roll back onto my stomach and hold my upper body up by putting my elbows on the bed. Scooping up a big heaping spoonful of mac-n-cheese, I groan.

"Good?"

"Mm-hm. Good," I say with my mouth full. Kennedy is back with my milk and a small plate of her own food. "Sit." I pat the bed. "Want to watch something?"

"In a second. I want to get ice for your rump."

She leaves again, returning with a Ziploc baggy full of ice. When she sets it on my ass, I jump. "Cold." I chuckle.

"Here, take these," she says, holding out two pills. "Anti-inflammatory medicine."

I take them from her hand and toss them back, swallowing them right along with the milk. "Sit," I say, patting the bed again. She remains standing next to my bed as she takes a bite of chicken. She's acting weird. "Kennedy?"

"Uh, right." She moves around to the other side of the bed and sits on the edge. I want her closer, but I'll take what I can get.

"The television remote is next to you on the nightstand."

"What do you want to watch?"

"Whatever you want to watch," I say, meaning every word.

"You're the patient, Ernie. You get to pick."

"Maybe there's a Cubs game on?" I think she likes the Cubs. I've seen her wear a Cubs T-shirt to work.

"Ooh, yeah. Let's see." She clicks around until she finds a game. "They're going to make the playoffs again."

"I hope so. A repeat would be cool."

"Very." She sits back on my bed with her back against my headboard. I grab a pillow for her to tuck behind her, so she's not leaning on wood. "Thanks," she says with a mouth full of cheesy noodles.

Since I'm facing away from the television, I move around so my feet are against the headboard and my head is at the foot of my bed. We eat in companionable silence as we watch the game. It feels good, right. When I feel her hand on my leg, I want to moan. She's doing it absently; I can tell because she's moving it back and forth over my leg like someone does to soothe or comfort someone else. But, for me, it's a turn on. Anytime Kennedy touches me, it makes me hard. When her little hand moves up behind my knee to the start of my thigh, I can't hold back. I moan.

"Feel good?"

"Yeah. I love your hands on me."

"You do?"

"Fuck, yeah, Kennedy. I wish...." I hesitate.

"Wish what?'

"I like it when you're with me."

"I do too, Ernie. It's just...." She pauses, setting her uneaten dinner on the nightstand. "I'm not looking for a serious rela-tionship."

I turn my body to my side to face her. "I wasn't either, Kennedy, believe me. But now, that's all I want—with you."

Sighing, she stops stroking my leg. Damn it. It felt so good. "Don't stop." I look down at her hand.

She slides out of bed. "You finished eating?"

"Yeah," I say, defeated. I move back up, so my head is at the top of my bed. I guess this whole thing tonight with Kennedy is over. When she slides back into bed, my head jerks up in surprise. "You're still here?"

"Yeah. Unless you want me to go."

"No. I want you here." *Always.*

She reaches over and switches off the lamp next to her and scoots down in the bed. "I want you to take tomorrow off."

"Why?"

"To heal your, uh, ass. If anyone asks, I'll tell them you're with your dad. Now," she says, patting her lap, "come on. Put your head here."

I move over and rest my head on her soft lap. When I feel her fingers run through my hair, I expel a sigh of relief. "Feels good."

"I like your haircut. Did I mention that?"

"No. But I'm glad." *I did it for you.*

"It was cute longer too. You've got a face that can pull off longer hair."

"Thanks." I turn and look back at her. "Which do you like better? Long or short?"

"Hmm...." She taps her chin and smiles. "I do like them both, but it was hot longer. I could picture you with it pulled back."

"Like my cousin Mick's hair used to be?"

"Yeah. You're a Flynn. You'll look foxy no matter what."

"Foxy?" I laugh.

"Yep. Foxy."

I chuckle and lay my head back down. "You're a fox too, Kennedy."

"I've got the red hair." She snorts.

"True. But I'd go so far as to say that 'foxy' doesn't do you justice."

"Oh, yeah? Then, what, pray tell, is better than 'foxy'?"

"Fucking beautiful."

Her fingers pause in my hair for a second, but they start back up again. "Thank you, Ernie," she whispers.

"It's true," I whisper back. "It's the absolute fucking truth." This time I squeeze her knee gently with my hand.

I grow sleepy feeling her fingers slide through my hair. I don't remember a time when I've felt this loved. Maybe before Mom died. Kennedy has that quality about her. Like she loves and cares like a mother. Kennedy's more than that though. She's complicated. On the one hand, she's bossy and so fucking dominant; on the other, she's a nurturer. She's the best of both worlds.

16
——————

## PLAN D



I'm having the most delicious dream. I moan aloud; it's so real. When I feel pressure between my legs, I realize it's not a dream. It's very real. Ernie Flynn's going down on me like it's his goddamn job. "Ernie?" It's still dark, maybe the middle of the night. Who knows? Who *cares*?

"Shh, babe. Lie back and relax."

"Relax? Good luck with that. Oh, oh, oh...." He's got me so turned on thanks to that wicked tongue of his and those huge fingers. "Ernie," I say with a whiny voice. "You're such a good boy."

"I aim to please my woman," he says proudly. "You taste so good, Kennedy."

I grab his hair and push him back down. "Less talking. More of whatever you were doing."

He chuckles and dives back in. He does this thing with his finger, I'm not sure what, but it makes me come like a rocket. "Oh, wow! That was different."

"Let's do it again."

"I...." I can't speak because he's right back to work. Okay. Good. This is good. He works me into a frenzy, and. I'm pressing into him with such force I may suffocate him, but he's moaning into me. I'm going to take that as a positive.

When I launch again, he pulls back, smiling. "Good?"

"Oh, yeah." I reach down until I make contact with his dick. I grasp it the best I can and pump up and down slowly.

He moves up further until we're face-to-face. When he kisses me softly, I taste myself. His mouth quickly turns ravenous as he works my lips open with his tongue. He maneuvers his body a little more so he can slide between my legs. He uses his big thigh to open me up wider to make room for him. "I want you so much, Kennedy."

He trails kisses down my neck, but my T-shirt's in the way, so he moves his mouth over my nipple and sucks on it through the shirt. I arch my back. The sensation is unreal. The next thing I know, the tee is up around my neck, above my breasts, and he's latched onto the same nipple while he pinches the other one. I love it. My nipples are extra sensitive today. I think I could come from his hand and mouth. I whimper like a frigging puppy. "Ernie." It feels so good.

My head is pushed back into my pillow as I feel his hands rustling around between my legs. When I feel something pressing into me, I hold my breath. His fingers pump into my wetness as his thumb circles my overly sensitive clit. I'm seconds from exploding. "You've got the tightest pussy, Kennedy. Such a sweet, little clit. Do you like this? You like what I'm doing to you, princess?"

"Yeah. Shit, yes," I hiss as my channel clamps down on his fingers.

"I want to fuck you so hard. You want that too?"

I nod frantically, and that's when it happens for the third time tonight. This time when I come, it sends a calming sensation through my entire body. It's like I'm boneless.

"You want my cock, Kennedy?"

"Yeah," I say lazily.

He thrusts into me with one hard push, and I feel like he's splitting me in half.

"Fuck, you're perfect!" he groans.

He stops moving. He's planted inside me and is sitting completely still.

"Move. I need you to move. Go, go, go, Ernie." I'm so drenched; he slides out easily. His next thrust is hard and fast. "Oh, hell," I moan. "More. Harder." Yeah, I'm a demanding bitch.

He places his hands on my ass and nudges me up a little bit and plunges in deep, hitting a spot that sends me into space. Is that my spot? I squeak and pump my hips upward in the hopes he'll hit it again. He does.

"Oh, Ernie. God, don't stop. I'm gonna come so hard. Don't stop."

"I won't, princess. Come for me. Come on, you can do it." I come hard, screaming out his name. Holy hell. I'm pulsing around his dick so hard and fast I feel a tiny tremor of another orgasm. How many was that? Five?

"Wow, Ernie. That... that was fantastic." I feel him plant inside me. He arches his back and shouts my name out as he throbs inside of me. I can almost feel him coming inside the condom; it's that powerful.

Ernie's taking in deep gulps of air, but I see his smile even in the dark of the night thanks to the light that's coming through his window. As he slowly pulls out, I feel wetness between my legs. I don't remember ever being that wet before. I reach down, and it hits me. "Ernie?"

"Yeah, princess?"

"Uh, did you wear a condom?" Silence. More silence. So much silence it's deafening. "Ernie?"

"No," he says so softly I barely hear him.

"What?" I shout. I sit up in his bed and feel more of him escaping my body. "What did you say?

"No. I didn't wear a—"

I jump out of bed and race into his bathroom, looking for my clothes. "I can't believe this." I'm muttering to myself but loud enough for him to hear. *Am I close to ovulating? Fuck!*

"Kennedy, I—"

"Fuck. Not again."

"Not again, what?" he asks, sounding panicked.

I pull on my dirty work pants, then my shirt, buttoning it up and missing buttons as I go, foregoing the bra and panties I can't find. "Who gave you permission to enter me without a condom, Ernie?"

"Uh, you...."

"Me? I gave you permission? Did we use condoms at my house?"

"Yes."

"So what made you think I would let you fuck me bare?"

"It's just...."

"Just what?" I scream directly up at his face.

He says nothing. He stands in his living room naked with his mouth hanging open.

"When you're off tomorrow. I want you to go to your doctor and get tested. As soon as you get the results, I want them. You got me?"

"I've got—"

"Until then, you don't talk to me unless I speak to you first. Do. You. Understand?"

He nods. His head falls forward onto his chest. Jesus, he looks like a sad little boy.

Tough shit.

I turn and grab his doorknob. Pulling it open, it strikes me. I've got it. Plan D, and it's *Hey, guess what, Ernie? You're gonna be a daddy.* Yeah, that'll work like a charm. Because I know, first-hand, guys don't stick around when shit gets real.

I walk out and slam the door behind me. Standing outside his apartment door, I run my fingers through my tangled hair and yell, *"Fuuuuuck!"* right before I stomp down the steps and out of Ernie Flynn's fucking life.

———

# 17

## WTF?

ERNIE

What the fuck just happened? Okay, I know I shouldn't have gone bare, and I definitely shouldn't have come inside her. I've screwed plenty of women bare, but I always pulled out. Not this time though. No, this time I pressed in as far as fucking possible. It was like I wanted to plant my seed or something. Still standing in my living room still staring at my door, I run my fingers through my short hair. Tonight was perfect. I don't remember ever feeling that comfortable with someone. I wanted to stay in my bed with Kennedy Corcoran forever. But I fucked it up.

I turn back to my bedroom and fall face-first on to my bed. I lift my head up to look at the clock on my nightstand. Three thirty in the morning. Kennedy was upset and driving in the middle of the night. I reach out for my phone to text her.

**Me**: I know you're pissed but send me a quick text to let me know you're home safe.

I set the phone next to my head and stare at it. At this time of night, it'll take her fifteen minutes to get home. She'll need to park and walk into her house. So, I'll give her thirty minutes before I call her. Drowsy, I close my eyes for a few minutes, but I'm awoken to a text.

**Kennedy:** I'm home.

That's it? That's all she's going to say? I pick my phone up and send another one.

**Me:** I'm sorry, Kennedy. I'll go to my doctor tomorrow. I'm sure I'm clean, but I'll get proof so you can rest easy.

I wait for a response, but when I get none, I decide she's most likely already back in her bed. I fall asleep worrying about her and about us and whether or not there's even an "us" anymore. Doubtful. She was pretty pissed.

18

# COINCIDENCES

ERNIE

I wake up on my own at 7:40 a.m. Blinking away the morning haze, I remember the events from the previous night and groan. I recall what I need to do today. I slide out of bed, waiting for pain, but my ass feels a lot better. I pull my boxers down and check out my injuries in the bathroom mirror. There are still some pink lines, but the welts are gone. I touch one of the spots with my finger, and it feels fine.

Making coffee and searching for something for breakfast, I spy the leftovers from the food Kennedy brought over. I grab the mac-n-cheese and nuke it in the microwave. When I pull it out, I see the cheese bubbling on the surface. I sink a fork in and bite. I love leftovers. I think food actually tastes better the next day. The flavors soak in overnight. By the time I've eaten and finished off one cup of coffee, it's eight. It means I can call Dr. Merkle's office and hope he's got an opening or a cancellation. When my favorite receptionist of all time answers, I clear my throat and say, "Uh, yes. I was wondering if Dr. Merkle had any time to see me today."

"Who is this?" she says curtly.

"Ernest Flynn."

I hear clicking in the background.

"Nope. He's booked solid."

Fuck. "I need to get in today. I—"

"He's booked. I told you that."

Frustration is setting in because this woman won't listen. "Is there someone else at the clinic?"

"What's the problem?"

*It's none of your business.* That's what I'd like to say, but I remain cool, calm, and collected. "I need some tests run."

"What kind of tests?"

This woman.... "STD tests, *ma'am*," I emphasize the ma'am part because, well, because.

"Oh."

I wait for something. More clicking. Something. But what I hear is whispering. That's not good. "Hello?"

Sighing, she finally speaks, "Can you be here at 8:30?"

I look up at the clock. It's almost eight ten. "I'll try."

"Try hard." Then I hear a click.

I jump up, open my dresser, and pull out a pair of clean sweatpants. I dig around another drawer and select a sweatshirt. Slipping on flip-flops from the corner of my room, I grab my wallet and keys, and then I'm out the door in less than five minutes. This time of morning, traffic is crazy. I weave in and out as fast as I can. If I miss my appointment, I'll have to figure out a plan B. At 8:29, I pull into the clinic parking lot. I jump out of the car and jog up to the front door. I yank the door open and nearly run into someone. I start to make my apologies for nearly running this person down when I see who it is.

"Oh, hey," I say softly. "How... how are you? How's Ashley?" I look around for the little beauty, but she's not there. A lump seems to clog my airways.

"She's hanging in there," says her mom, smiling. "She's with my mom today."

I blink at her, waiting for more.

"I came in to see about some test results."

"Test results?" This is none of my business. I know that, but for some reason, I feel connected to this woman and Ashley.

"Bone marrow. We were hoping for a match. Ashley's leukemia is, uh, it's not going well."

"Leukemia?"

She nods.

"I've never asked, but what's your name?"

"Penny. Penny Boggs."

I raise my hand to shake hers. "I'm Ernie Flynn. Can you please tell Ashley I said hello?"

Penny Boggs gives me a bright smile. "I will. She'll be disappointed she missed you. She talks about you whenever we come here. And we come here a lot."

"I think about her too... and you." I reflect on that day in the hallway when she slowly shook her head. It hurt in my chest. "Well, I'm running late so...."

"See you around, Ernie Flynn," she says, squeezing my forearm.

Nodding, I move into the office and walk briskly up to Cruella DeVille. "I'm here."

"I see that. You're late."

I blink at her, hoping she laughs or something, but I get nothing. Keeping my irritation in check, I reply, "It's rush hour. I got here as fast as I could."

"Have a seat. We'll get to you soon."

Get to me? "Jesus," I mutter. I plop down in front of the television that's playing some stupid talk show. I watch the show, but I don't listen. I think about Ashley and Penny instead. That sweet girl shouldn't have to go through this shit.

After about twenty minutes, I hear my name. I jump up and walk quickly to Dr. Merkle's nurse. At the scale, I see I'm down another ten pounds from my last visit. I know I've built up muscle, so that ten pounds is more than ten pounds of fat. I smile at the number on the scale and follow her back to an exam room. Inside, she asks me why I'm there. I came up with the answer on the ride over. "I've started seeing someone. I want to be sure I'm clean before, uh, before...." Pure genius. Now I don't sound like a fucking irresponsible asshole that fucks a girl bare, then lets loose inside her. That'd be an asshole move, for sure. *Ugh.*

"All right. I'll take your vitals, and we'll let the doctor figure what you'll need. Sound good?"

Doc Merkle is pleased with my story too. "That's very responsible of you, Ernie. Glad to know you learned something from the last, uh, episode."

"Uh-huh. I sure did." *God, I suck.*

He does every test, including a throat swab and a dick swab (don't ask). I give him a urine sample, and while he jots the order for the blood tests, I cleared my throat and ask, "So, uh, Doc?"

"Yes," he says absently.

"What do you need to do to find out if you're a match for someone who needs a bone marrow transplant?"

His head jerks up, and he blinks at me. "What?"

"Bone marrow. How do I find out if I'm a match for someone?"

"Who? Who needs your bone marrow?"

"Ashley Boggs."

"I know her." He nods. "How do *you* know her?"

Not that it's any of his business. "From around."

"I see. Do you want to be tested to see if you're a match?"

I nod slightly. "I think so. What do I need to do for that?"

"We draw blood. But your insurance may not cover the lab work. Plus, if you're a match, they may not cover the transplant procedure. You may want to check with them first."

"Nah. That's fine. I'll risk it." Ashley's life is definitely worth it. I've got money coming in now. I can pull from savings if I need to. My dad will pitch in if I absolutely needed help. "I'll be all right." I nod.

"Great. I'll order those tests along with these others," Dr. Merkle says as he smiles at me—like he's proud of me. "Sit tight. A nurse will be in to draw your blood. I'll let you know the results as soon as they come in. Sound good?"

"Sure." I wait for a few minutes.

When the door opens, a pretty, young woman walks in smiling brightly. "Ernie Flynn?"

"Yep."

"I'm here to draw blood."

"Okay. Sounds good."

"You're getting tested for Ashley?"

"Yeah. You know her?"

"We all do. She's here a lot. She's a cool little girl."

"That she is."

She clears her throat, and I see her eyes shining with wetness. "I think what you're doing is so amazing."

"I haven't done anything yet."

"I know. It's just cool."

*Cool? I'm not cool. I'm an asshat.* "Thanks." I remain quiet while the nurse draws blood. I can't watch the procedure, so I look up at the ceiling.

"All done."

"I look down and see a SpongeBob bandage on my arm, and I chuckle. "Nice."

"Sorry. It was between that and Dora the Explorer. I thought SpongeBob was more masculine.

"Good choice." I hop off the table and make my way to the door.

"Ernie?"

I turn to the girl. "My name's Kate. If, uh, you ever...."

"Thanks. You're a cute girl, but I've found my...." I hesitate. *My what?*

"You've found your future?"

I smile at that idea. I like it. "I have."

"Lucky girl."

"I'm the lucky one."

Walking out the door, I check out with Cruella and walk out into the cool autumn air. My day is completely open now—I've got no plans. I could do whatever I want, but all I want to do is see Kennedy. Since that's not happening, I call my dad to see if he wants to meet up for dinner. It's time for me to get some advice from my wise, old dad.

# FRIDAYS SUCK UNTIL THEY DON'T

## KENNEDY

Ugh, Friday's *suck*. The guys are fucking up left and right; I've got no patience for it. I've screamed at Dave, Phil, Lester, and now it's Timmy's turn. I should feel sorry for Timmy, but he's on my last nerve.

"Goddamn it, Timmy!" I screech. "You aren't authorized to work the backhoe." He has no idea how to operate the fucking sixteen-thousand-pound digger. I watch him lift the bucket up at Mach speed and slam it back to the ground, missing the edge of the building by inches.

"But Jake said I could try it."

I look over at Jake, the *real* heavy equipment operator. I give him my best glare. Jake's a big guy at about six two and way over two hundred and fifty pounds. He isn't intimidated easily. So, Jake glares back. When I step toward him, he backs down. I turn back to Timmy. "Oh, I see." I turn to walk away but stop and turn back. I look up at him in his perch in the driver's seat. "So, Jake's gonna sign your check?"

"N-No."

"Jake? Are you going to sign his check?"

"Nope," he says with his arms crossed over his massive chest.

I continue to look at him. "Are you going to sign your own check?"

He slowly moves his arms down to his side, flexing his fists as he goes. I'm not scared. My brothers do that kind of shit all the time. It's intended to frighten me, but I know for a fact he'd never hit me—and not because I'm a woman. It's because his wife is my best friend and she'd kick his ass from here to Naperville.

Knowing all of this, he finally murmurs, "No."

I slam my fists on my hips and move closer to Jake. "Then, I suggest you help little Timmy down from there and remember that there are laws, codes, regulations, and safety concerns for letting a dipshit like Timmy behind the wheel of heavy machinery. Are we clear?"

"We're clear," he growls.

"Good." I turn in the direction of my trailer. As I go, I yell, "Get back to work, fuckers!"

When I turn the corner on my way back to my office, I lift my head and see a stunning man waving at me. Brock Lancaster is leaning on my office door, looking hot as sin in some tight jeans and a snug Chicago Blackhawks tee. My God, that man is beautiful.

As I approach him, I hear him chuckling. "You run a tight ship here, Kennedy." When I reach him, he stands up at his full height. Looking down at me, he gives me a beaming smile.

"I try. But it's not easy with some of these dipshits." I point my thumb back toward Timmy.

"I know what you mean. Surrounded by fools and idiots most of the time myself."

It's my turn to laugh. "Mind if I use that one? It fits."

"Be my guest."

"So, what can I do for you? I know we passed the initial inspection."

"I came by to see what you're doing tonight."

What I'm doing tonight? Is he asking me out? "Uh, no plans, why?"

He steps a little closer to me. So close I can smell his after-shave. I can tell it's something fancy and manly, but nice. I lean in a bit to get another whiff. "I need a date tonight. Going to a stupid awards banquet. I hate going to those things, and going alone stinks."

I groan. "An awards banquet? Those suck, Brock."

He throws his head back and laughs loudly. "They do. What if I promised you we'd leave right after my category? I'll take you to an Irish pub for some Guinness and fish 'n' chips.

"Wow, you remembered?" I love me some Irish pubs, fish 'n' chips, and Guinness.

"Of course."

"You're nominated for an award?"

"It's nothing important—City of Chicago employee of the year. I'm one of ten nominees. It's a new thing they're doing to improve morale." He looks at me with sad eyes, fluttering his lashes. "Please, Kennedy?"

"Are you seriously giving me sad eyes?"

"Is it working?"

"No!" I say as I laugh. "Yes." I point my finger up at him. "But there'd better be an Irish pub afterward or your name is mud."

He places his big hand over his even bigger chest. "Cross my heart, honey. I won't let you down."

"All right. What time? Is this thing formal?" I groan again, thinking about wearing heels and shit.

"I'll pick you up at six. It's not formal, but think cocktail dress."

"Cocktail dress. Six." Jesus, do I have a cocktail dress?

He moves a rogue strand of hair out of my eyes. "See you then. I can't wait." He leans down to give me a kiss on the cheek.

A shiver runs from my cheek, down my neck, over my nipple, and straight down to hoo-ha land. Damn, he smells amazing. This Friday started off sucktastically, but things have definitely turned around. Yes. They. Have.

I smile through the rest of the day. I even talk Dave into taking over so I can cut out a little early. I need to get myself a cocktail dress and still get home and attempt to make myself presentable. Wish me luck.

# DAD KNOWS BEST

## ERNIE

"Sorry I'm late," says my dad as he slides into the booth.

"No problem. I eat late most nights anyway." I pick up the menu and ask, "What's good here?" My dad loves Mrs. Murphy and Sons Irish Bistro. He comes here once a week. Apparently, my Grandmother Flynn and Mrs. Murphy were best friends, or so the story goes.

"Well, it's Friday, so they've got seafood stew and homemade bread. That's what I'm getting," he says, rubbing his hands together like he can't wait.

"Hmm, that sounds interesting." This place is super traditional Irish food from shepherd's pie to scotch eggs. "I think I'm going to get bangers and mash. I haven't had that for years." Bangers are Irish sausages while mash is mashed potatoes. It's fucking delicious.

"It's good here too. They stick with tradition," he says with pride.

After we order, the server brings us our beers. Dad's quietly sipping his beer, and I'm wondering if I should be telling him about Kennedy. He's technically her boss. I'd hate to cause her any grief, but he's my dad first, and he gives the best advice.

"So, why am I here?" He chuckles.

"Well, I did something today."

"Okay...," he says cautiously.

"I had a blood test to see if I'm a bone marrow match for a little girl I met at the doctor's office." I say all of that without breathing.

"Bone marrow?"

I suck in air and start over. I tell him all about Ashley and Penny Boggs. I explain about the blood tests and the possible procedure and the costs. "I don't think I'll need any help paying for it, but I may."

I've been staring at the table while I explain my situation, so when I look up at my dad, I'm a little shocked to see tears running down his face. "Dad? What's wrong? Did I do something wrong? Jesus!"

He shakes his head and uses the back of his hand to wipe away the wetness on his face. "No, absolutely not! It's, uh, I don't think I've ever been prouder of you, Ernie. That's such a kind, amazingly generous thing you're doing for that family. Of course, I'll help you. I'd be proud to contribute. Hell, I may even get tested myself if you aren't a match."

I'm humbled by his reaction. So much so the only thing I can say is "Thanks, Dad."

When our food is delivered, we're quiet for a good long time. We're both hungry, and when the guys in my family are hungry, eating comes first, talking second. When I'm about a third of the way through, I lift my glass of beer up to my mouth. Taking a big gulp, I see something red in my peripheral vision. *That fucking hair.*

I start to choke and nearly spit out the contents of my mouth. "What the fuck?" I slam the glass down on the table. "What the hell is she doing with *him*?" I pound my fist on the table once, which causes a chain reaction. First, my glass tips over, bumping Dad's as it goes. His glass tips into his bowl of stew, essentially ruining his dinner. Mine ends up all over the table.

I slide out of the booth and move quickly to the bar. When I reach her, she's ordering something from a server, but I don't give a fuck. "What are you doing here with *him?*" I point to the douchebag in the suit sitting across from Kennedy.

I don't even give the asshole the honor of my glare because I never take my eyes off her. She looks fucking gorgeous in a slinky black dress that shows way too much cleavage. My eyes keep moving downward. It's another one of those dresses that ties at her waist, but this one has a slit showing a whole fuck ton of bare leg. I move down to her feet and see some sexy-as-hell spiked heels. They've got to be four inches high.

I jerk my head back up to her face. She's got on a lot of makeup. Too damn much makeup. Her lips are glossy and cherry red, and her hair is amazing. It's still curly, but they aren't tight curls. Tonight, they're in big waves that flow down her back. Kennedy glares at me. It's a look I've seen before. She's already pissed, and I just got here. I couldn't give two shits. "You're on a fucking date?"

A big dude in an apron approaches me. "Sir, you're disturbing the other patrons."

I turn to the apron guy. "I found my woman on a date with this fucktard." I jerk my thumb toward the plumbing inspector, Blake something or other.

He looks from me to that guy and glares at him. "Keep it down," he mutters as he returns to wherever he came from.

I turn back to Kennedy. "Well?"

"Well what, Ernie?"

"Why are you out on a date with this dipshit?"

"Because he asked me."

I'm practically beside myself with that comment. "Because he *asked* you?"

"Yes."

"Because he *asked* you?" My voice is getting loud again. "Kennedy, we need to talk."

"Not right now. Maybe later," she says dismissively.

I'm so... so fucking jealous. I feel like my head's going to explode. "Kennedy Corcoran—"

"Son?" A big palm rests on my shoulder. "Let's go."

"No. Dad, she's mine." I point to Kennedy. "She's—"

"Your girl?" scoffs the fuckwit named Brad or some shit.

I turn slowly toward him. "She's. My. *Future!*" I shout this time.

"Your future? *I'm* your future?" Kennedy whispers.

I turn back to her. She looks a little shocked or something. I can't describe the look. All I can say is her face isn't angry anymore. It's sort of soft. "Yeah. You're my woman. You're my soul mate, I know it." I know I sound like a fucking pussy, but I couldn't care less.

"Ernie, we barely know each other."

"I knew the first day I started work you were the one."

"There's no such thing as love at first sight, Ernie."

My dad interjects then. "I beg to differ, Kenny. I fell in love with my Rachel the day I set eyes on her. Ethan? Same thing. When he saw Claire, he was a goner. It's in our blood."

She opens her mouth then closes it. When she opens it again to speak, the douche interrupts. "Well, she's on a date with me, so I guess you can see you're not *her* future."

I raise my fist. I'd love to punch this guy's face off. "Ernie? No!" Kennedy shouts. She slides off her stool and moves to me. Placing her palm on my angry fist, she pushes it down. "Go home, Ernie. I'll call you later. We can talk about everything then, okay?"

I look down into her golden eyes. "You're staying? You're going to remain on this *date?*" I spit the word date out.

"I am. We're old friends. We're catching up."

"Catching up?"

"Yeah. We went to college together."

I'm pissed. What the fuck does "catching up" mean? Were they lovers? Is that why she said "not again" last night? Was he the reason for that statement? I can barely hold it together. I want to hit something, and I want to cry too.

My dad places his hand on my shoulder again. "Come on, Ern. Let's go."

I slump my shoulders and turn, following him out the door. As soon as we make it outside and around the corner, I lose it. Dad wraps his big arms around me and holds me. Yeah, you don't need to say it. I already know I'm acting like a pussy.

"Son, it's going to be okay. These things happen. Have faith that it'll work out. If she's yours, then it'll happen. Patience is needed in this case. Kennedy's a tough nut to crack, but if anyone can do it, it's you, Ernie."

I pull away from him, wiping my face. "I've never felt this way before. It's messing with my head."

"I know. I was there."

"Did you actually fall for Mom the first time you met her?"

"I did. She wasn't easy to catch either. The good ones aren't. It's better if you have to work for it. It helps you see how precious it is once she's yours. You appreciate her more. You never take her for granted."

My dad's face looks sad. He lost his wife, my mom, eighteen years ago. I don't think he's ever dated another person in all those years. I wish he would, though. He deserves a good woman. "Thanks, Dad. You had my back. I needed that."

He slaps my back a little too hard. "You'd do the same for me, I'm sure."

"Are you upset about me and Kennedy?"

"Not upset. Surprised. You usually go for the anorexic blonde type. But Kennedy Corcoran is a keeper. That's for damn sure. I'm pleased with your choice. I couldn't have chosen better for you." He pats my shoulder again. "Now, let's go home. I'm beat."

"Me too." But going home alone sucks. It's Friday night, and I wish.... Oh, fuck it. I'll pick up a six-pack and some pizza, since I didn't get to finish my dinner. I'll drink and eat my sorrows away. Maybe some Ben and Jerry's too.

"Love you, Ern."

"Love you too, Dad. Thanks again."

He nods as he slides into his car. I do the same. Time to go home. Alone.

## MY GIRL



"Wow, that was something, wasn't it?"

I'm pulled from my daze. "Huh?" I let out a relieved laugh. "Yeah, that was something."

Brock chuckles absently. "Your *future?* Who says that bullshit?"

I look up at him as he opens up his menu. "Right?" I say, sounding completely in agreement. To be honest, the phrase is one I've used since I was in high school. I think it's something my mom used to say about my dad. She'd say, "*I knew Herb was my future the minute he said hello to me.*" But, Ernie? Does Ernie actually think *I'm* his? Is *he* mine?

"Are you listening, Kenny?"

Pulled from those thoughts again by Brock, I blink. "Sorry. What were you saying?"

Brock sighs impatiently. "Are you still thinking about that dumbass?"

"He's not dumb. He's brilliant, actually." And sweet and gorgeous and a frigging dynamo in bed.

"You don't have to be dumb to be a dumbass."

That caught my attention and made me laugh. "Amen!" I

lift my glass of delicious Guinness. Before I take a sip, I remember last night with Ernie. Condomless Ernie. I set the glass down. "You know what? I'm in the mood for something nonalcoholic tonight."

"You are? You're passing up the 'Nectar of the Gods'?"

"You remember that too?"

Brock reaches over and places his hand on top of mine. "I remember everything, Kennedy. I had such a crush on you in college."

"You did not!" I giggle. "No way. You were always all over Stacy Hart."

"Yeah, well, I always had my eye on you," he says, squeezing my hand.

I don't believe it. Not for a second. Brock Lancaster and Stacy Hart were caught, multiple times, doing it in various nooks and crannies at the university. I don't think they ever did it in their own apartments. "Did you two ever do it at home?" I look over at him as he blushes. It's kind of cute.

"Yeah, we, uh, had a thing for public...." He doesn't finish the sentence, but I get it.

"Ah, I see. To each his own." I lift my glass again to feign a toast. Fuck, I can't drink. What if I'm pregnant? When a server walks by, I raise my hand. When they look my way, I ask, "Can I get a glass of water?" The server smiles and nods.

When she returns with my water, we order dinner. "I'll have the fish 'n' chips," I say, although my appetite left with Ernie.

"I'll have the Caesar salad, no dressing or croutons."

"Uh, are you on a diet?" I ask, totally shocked by his order.

"I thought we'd share our food. You shouldn't eat an entire order of fish 'n' chips."

"Why not?" Oh, I *know* why not, but let's see what old Brock has to say.

"Well, I think you're beautiful, Kennedy, but you have to admit you've put on a little weight since college."

"Actually, *Brock,* I've lost fifteen pounds since college." Working on a construction site, you burn a lot of calories.

"Huh," he says absently. "Well, good for you." He lifts his glass. My glass remains on the table.

"I hate when guys do that." I slide off my stool.

"Do what?"

"That passive-aggressive diet bullshit. I happen to think I'm fucking sexy as hell, naked or dressed."

"You are!" he practically squeaks. "You're fucking hot, Kenny."

I reach over and grab my purse. "Thanks for tonight. It was great catching up with you, Brock." I pat his arm. "See you around."

"But... but...."

I don't stop walking until I'm out the door and down the street. I need a taxi, but I want to get away from the restaurant, so Brock doesn't come out and try to sweet talk me into going back inside. "Guys can be such dicks," I grumble.

When the cab screeches to a halt in front of me, I open the door and slide inside, reciting my address as I go. Drawing in air to my lungs, I sigh. "What a night." Laying my head back onto the headrest, I squeeze my eyes shut. The awards banquet was as boring as I assumed it would be. Brock actually won the award. I think he knew he was going to win. He had a speech prepared. He didn't get to make it though, because they were trying to wrap it up, so he said, "thank you," and stepped off the stage. I think he was pretty bummed he didn't get to talk. Oh well, there's always next year.

As the cab pulls up in front of my house, I hand the man cash for the ride. I slide out, stepping on a strip of grass in front of my house. My heels sink into the dirt a little bit, but I'm able to navigate it easily enough. Straightening my dress as I step on the sidewalk, I look down at the mud on my new heels. "Fucking great," I mutter. I'll clean them off as soon as I get inside.

Clicking up my front walk to my steps, I reach into my purse for my keys. It's a tiny bag, but my keys are evading capture.

"Have fun tonight?" a deep voice to my left says.

Startled, I step backward and lose my balance. Grasping hold of the wooden railing, I keep myself from landing ass over tit. "What the fuck, Ernie! You scared the bejesus out of me!"

"Sorry."

He's not sorry. "Why are you here?"

He stands up from one of my wicker chairs and stalks toward me. "I wanted to see if you brought him home."

"Ernie," I growl.

He hasn't stopped walking. He walks right up to me, pressing his broad chest into mine until I'm forced to back up. When my ass hits the railing, Ernie brings his arms up and places his hands on the top of the railing on either side of my hips. "I had to know," he says an inch from my mouth.

"Know what?" I know what he wanted to know.

"I wanted to know if you were going to fuck him."

"That's none—" I don't get the rest of the words out because Ernie's mouth tastes mine hungrily. I make a feeble attempt to pull away, but it lasts only a second or two. When he sweeps his tongue into my mouth, I'm a goner. I bring my arms up to wrap around his neck and to pull me up into him. My nipples are hard, and I'm fast becoming turned on to the point of no return.

I slide my leg up his until I've got it wrapped around his hip. As he presses into my stomach, I slide my hands down, searching for his belt, but he pulls away. Like completely away.

He steps back at least two feet while I stand with my back against the hard wooden rail, panting like I ran a marathon.

I watch him turn slightly and walk toward the steps. "What? What're you doing?"

"I'm going home."

"Home? Why?"

Ernie scoffs. "When you figure out you want to be with me and *only me*, call me. Until then, this," he says, pointing back and forth between us, "is on hold."

"On hold?" I screech.

He steps down onto my front walk and away from me. "Ernie Flynn!" I shout, "You get back here right this minute!" He'll listen. He loves my bossiness. When he doesn't turn around, I shout, "You're a very bad boy!"

He stops walking and turns back to face me. There's indecision on his face. I see it. And anger, there's anger too. He stomps back up my steps and right back where he was before he made his stupid stand about us being *on hold*. He slides his hands into my hair and pulls my mouth to his. This kiss is way hotter than the first one, and it was sizzling hot.

"You want me to fuck you?"

"Yeah, I want that big cock, Ernie." I can feel it.

"Are you wet, Kennedy?" he says, sliding his hand up under my dress. I hold my breath, waiting for him to reach the promised land. When he does, he stops. *Oh, fuck.*

"You went on a date with that fucking dick, and you didn't wear panties?"

"Uh, it's not...." The truth is, they were damn uncomfortable. When I found this dress at one of my favorite little shops called Curvy Girl's, I thought it'd be fun to buy some new undies. I chose a thong. Without getting into too much detail, let me say, this thong was like a torture device. I've got a few thongs in my drawer, but they're stretchy and soft. These things? There was no give and the lace felt more like sandpaper than fabric. We didn't get along. But now Ernie thinks I did this because of Brock.

His hand jerks out of my dress so fast he nearly pulls me with it.

"Ernie?"

He starts to stomp away again. "They're in my purse. They're new. A thong. They were uncomfortable, so I took them off. I wasn't going pantyless for him. I swear!"

"Let me see them," he says, extending his arm toward me.

I reach into my bag and pull out the stringy undies from hell. He takes them from me and unfurls them. He brings them to his face and smells them. Oh shit, why is that so fucking hot? Next, Ernie kneels down in front of me, reaching for my ankle. When it's off the ground, he slides one opening of the thong up and around my foot and then repeats it with the other one.

Looking up at me, he slowly slides them up, up, up, until they're at the juncture of my legs. Standing, he brings the thong up with him until they're in place. Ugh, who can stand to wear these things? I feel like I'm being cut in half. He doesn't stop, though; he reaches for the tiny front triangle piece and pulls up. "Oh, fuck!" It's pressing on my clit, and it feels amazing.

He tugs several times, varying the pressure he's placing on me. I think I could come from this, but he stops suddenly. Gliding his palm down into the front, he brings his finger to my center and presses it in slowly. I moan so loud it's embarrassing. In and out his fingers move at a snail's pace. Every now and then, his thumb rubs my achy clit. I'm pressing my hips into his hand in an attempt to get more. "More, Ernie."

He works me until I'm practically salivating. Suddenly, he stops. "Who does this pussy belong to, Kennedy?"

Huh? My eyelashes flutter open as fast as a butterfly. "What?"

He slides his finger back inside. "I said, who does this pussy belong to?" After pulling his finger out, he pushes two back inside.

"Oh, God!"

Ernie stops again. "Tell me, Kennedy. Whose pussy is this?"

"Yours! Ernie, it's yours!" I wait for more, but what I get shocks me.

He steps back like he did before. I watch him bring his fingers to his mouth. He sucks and licks me from his fingers. Again, hot as hell. Walking to my steps, he stops and looks back at me, repeating, "When you're ready to be with me and *only* me, call me. Until then, this," he says, pointing back and forth between us again, "is on hold."

"Ernie?" I say weakly. He ignores me and keeps walking. "Ernie!" I say again more loudly. He's not coming back this time. I was seconds from coming all over his hand, and he stopped. For some reason, the whole thing with Ernie on my porch makes me smile. The bastard left me hangin'. So, now I'll spend the entire night thinking about him, his hand, and his big cock. I laugh to myself as I unlock my door.

"Well played, Flynn. Well played."

22

---

# I'M IN CHARGE NOW

ERNIE

When I get to work on Monday, J.C. is waiting for me. "You're with me today, Cherry."

"Seriously, when are you assholes going to stop calling me Cherry?" It should have stopped a week ago. They've hired someone since I started, but I'm still Cherry.

J.C. shrugs. "No clue. Come on, let's go." J.C. has been in the construction business for a hundred years. He started off like me, but he became a mason, better known as a bricklayer. He did that for most of his life, but now his back is too messed up to do it anymore. So, he supervises the masonry crew and the framing guys.

Since they're done doing the concrete block exterior, I'm led inside the cavernous building where about ten guys are carrying around long metal strips. They don't use wood for framing much anymore. Now they use galvanized steel studs instead. It's beneficial in this Midwestern climate because wood expands and contracts with the weather and various temperatures. Steel doesn't.

"You're going to be following Bud over there. He's going to show you the ropes."

I nod and walk over to Bud McKay. I've known him most of my life since he's an old friend of Dad's. "Hey, Bud."

"Hey, son. You workin' with me now?"

"I guess so. Tell me what to do."

Bud chuckles. "Sweet. Start bringing over the studs."

I walk over to one of the palettes holding the metal pieces. I lift one and realize it's light as air. I grab an armful and carry them to Bud.

"Don't carry so many, Ern. You can cut yourself on the edges, and they bend easily. So, about half that much in the future."

I nod and walk back to the pile. Grabbing half the load, I walk back. I spend the entire morning doing that as six other guys frame around the interior of the entire first floor. "This afternoon, we'll be upstairs. You'll be carrying those up then," says Bud at lunch.

"Okay. Sounds good."

"I'm surprised you're so amenable to manual labor, Ernie."

I stop moving as I'm about to bite into my PB&J. "What? Why?"

"I only remember you sitting at a computer or in front of the television playing video games. You barely spoke to anyone too."

"Yeah," I say solemnly, "I know. Sorry about that."

"Don't be sorry. It's just you."

It was. "Yeah, I guess." I shrug. I bite into my bland sandwich and chew. I've got to start bringing better lunches. I'm to the point now, if I see a jar of peanut butter, I want to puke.

Grabbing the chocolate bar I've got stashed at the bottom of my cooler, I raise my head and see Kenny walking across the site, straight to us. "Hey, guys. How's it going inside, Bud?"

"Good. Framed the exterior walls on the first floor. We're moving up to two after we eat."

"Wow, you made good time. That's great." She turns and

looks at me. She gives me a small smile that's kind of sweet. "Ernie? How's it going for you in there?"

"He's doing great," Bud interjects. "Donal would be proud."

She turns and gives me a real smile. "Really?"

"Why does that surprise you, pr—uh, Kenny?" I nearly called her "princess."

"No reason. You've been a tad difficult since you started here."

I stand and slam my cooler lid shut. "Difficult? Seriously?" I step toward her, crowding into her personal space. "I think I've been very *obedient*." I watch her face flush pink. It's beautiful.

"Ernie, knock it off," snips Bud. "She didn't mean anything by it."

I step back from her. "I know." I grab my cooler and stomp over to toss it with the rest of them. "I'm heading back in. I'll start taking the studs upstairs."

"Okay. See you in a few."

I grunt as I walk away. Part of me is extremely frustrated with her, part is turned the fuck on. I adjust myself in my pants so no one can see. Jesus, the smell of her makes me crazy. By two o'clock, the crew is nearly finished framing the second floor. These guys move so fucking fast. It's seriously amazing to watch. They're so in sync, they barely have to speak to one another.

"Ernie, why don't you start taking studs up to three?"

"Sure, Bud." There are only three floors to this building, so that'll be the highest I'll have to go. I don't mind, though. I feel my legs getting stronger from this workout, and I like it. With a full load in my arms, I stomp up to the landing on the third floor.

As I'm squatting down with the load, I hear someone scream. Let me clarify, I hear Kennedy scream. I drop the metal pieces and jerk to my feet. I hear more shouts and some cursing coming from the west side of the building. I run to the west side and peer out of an opening in the wall. Below me I see Kennedy lying flat on her back on the ground. Timmy is there, along with Dave and a couple other guys. I yell out the window, "Kennedy?"

Timmy isn't moving. He's standing there holding a pneumatic nail gun. Dave looks up and shouts, "Better get down here, Ernie."

I run as fast as I can, jumping over the studs I tossed to the ground. In thirty seconds, I'm on the first floor. I run out the door and around to the west. When I get there, J.C. is kneeling down beside her. I move to her other side and drop to my knees. "What happened?"

J.C. points to her hand. There's a nail sticking out of the center of her hand. It's pierced clean through. Blood is pooling in her palm and dripping onto the ground. "She's unconscious?"

"When she looked at her hand, she fainted," explains Dave.

I look at her face and see it's so pale it's practically white. Her hard hat is laying about a foot away from her. Did she hit her head? "Call 911!" I shout.

"We already did," J.C. says, looking concerned. "They're on their way."

I look up and see Timmy. He's still standing there clutching the nail gun. "You!" I yell, pointing accusingly at him. "You shot her with that?"

"It... it was an ac-accident," he stutters. "I didn't mean for the gun to go off." He pulls the hand up that's clutching the gun and wipes his cheek with the back of his hand. It's pointing right at me as he does it. "Put that fucking thing down!"

Tim blinks up and nods at me. Bending down, he places the nail gun at his feet. "I'm s-sorry. I didn't mean to hurt her. She's...."

She's what?

"Jesus, Tim. Get a grip," chides Dave. "She'll be okay. Kenny's a tank."

A tank? These guys all think she's so tough and strong, like she could withstand nail guns getting shot through her hand and hitting her head on this rocky ground? She's not. She's delicate. Like a flower. She's....

"What the hell?" she growls as she wakes up, attempting to sit up.

I push her back down. "Stay put. An ambulance is on its way."

"I don't need a fucking ambulance. I need to kick *his*"—she points at Timmy—"ass."

Dave and J.C. both chuckle. Timmy starts to blubber and cry again, while I stare down at her. "You need to lie still. You're going to the hospital to get checked out."

"No, I'm not," she says, trying to push herself up again. When she lifts her left hand that has the nail running through it, I see her swallow hard. "Fuck," she mutters.

"Yeah, you're going! It's company policy. Do I need to call my dad?"

I hear several guys make that "*ooooh*" sound, but I ignore it.

She gives up. "Fine. I'll go. But I'll be back, assholes!" she shouts, then winces and puts her good hand on the back of her head.

"Lie still," I repeat. "Or I'll carry you to my car and take you myself."

She glares at me then, which makes me laugh. I lean down and whisper in her ear, "It's your turn to follow orders, princess. I'm in charge now."

When we hear the sirens blasting from down the street, she grumbles, "Whatever. Let's get this over with."

# 23

# FML: PART DEUX

## KENNEDY

"So, Miss Corcoran, can you tell me how this happened?" The ER doctor is holding my hand up and turning it here and there like it's the oddest thing he's ever seen. I can't look at it. My stomach flips all over the place every time I see it.

"Well, one of the guys on my crew was screwing around with a pneumatic nail gun. You know, shooting it at shit on the ground."

"Uh-huh," he says absently.

"So, I went up to him and held my hand out, you know in a stopping motion." I demonstrate by holding my hand out to show the universal sign for Stop. "I must have startled him because he pulled the trigger right then and the nail shot into my hand." I swallow, attempting to make the feeling that I might vomit go away.

"Wow, that's some tale." He chuckles. "Well, let's get that out of there, shall we?"

"Do I need surgery?"

"Oh, heavens no. The X-ray shows you were fortunate; it missed all of the important stuff in your hand. We'll yank that sucker out of there."

I flinch at the words "yank that sucker out of there."

"Y-You're going to pull it out?"

"Of course. We'll numb your hand, so you won't feel a thing until after the numbing agent wears off."

"Then what?"

"It'll hurt. I'll give you a script for some pain meds so you can sleep." He types something into his laptop. Turning back to me, he shakes his finger at me. "No more playing with nail guns, missy." Then he giggles. Seriously. He giggles. "I'll be back in a few minutes. You sit tight."

"Huh?" *What just happened there?*

Before I can correct the weirdo, Ernie pokes his head into my little nook. "You've got company."

I look over at him as he pulls the curtain back. "Mom?"

"Oh, sweetie. How're you doing?"

"I'm good." I turn back to Ernie. "Uh, who else is here?"

"Your dad, one of your brothers." Ernie rolls his eyes. "My dad."

"Who called all of them?"

"Well, I called my dad. He called your parents."

"Ernie, why'd you call Donal?"

"Because you were hurt on the job. He needed to know."

"Whatever. I'm fine. They're going to 'yank the sucker out of there.'"

"Jesus," he mutters.

Yeah, *Jesus* is right. Before I can reply, Dr. Dork comes back into the room. "Miss Corcoran, do you remember the last time you had a tetanus shot?"

I close my eyes, trying to remember. "Those are the ones you need every ten years?"

"That's correct."

"I don't remember."

I look over at my mom, and she shrugs. "Middle school."

"Well, we'll go ahead and give you one of those along with some antibiotics. Are you allergic to any meds?"

"Not that I know of, Doc."

"Good," he says, typing into his computer. "Okay, is there any chance you could be pregnant?"

"What? Why do you need to know that?"

"Well, there are some things you shouldn't take if you're pregnant. The tetanus shot is fine if you're expecting, and some antibiotics are better than others. The pain medications could be a concern," he says absently.

He starts to turn, and I look down at my wounded paw and mumble, "There's a slight chance."

I hear a gasp, and I'm not sure which one of them did it—maybe both of them. "Kennedy?" They say simultaneously.

"What?" I snap at Ernie. "I told you...."

"You told me what? That you weren't on birth control? I don't think you mentioned that."

"Well, it was implied." *Or is that inferred? I can never keep those straight.*

"Implied my ass, sweetheart."

"Ernie Flynn!" my mom snaps. "Now you—"

Ernie holds his big hand up in that universal stopping sign I mentioned earlier. "With all due respect, Mrs. Corcoran, this is between Kennedy and me."

"Well...," she stutters. "All right." She sits back and places her hands in her lap and says nothing more.

He *is* the boss now. "Don't talk to my mom like that!"

"I meant no disrespect. This is between you and me, princess."

"Okay, so now you know. You can run away. I won't hold you accountable. If I am pregnant, you don't have to worry about—"

Ernie stomps over to me until his hips are against my bed.

He places his hand over my uninjured one and says, "Are you fucking kidding me right now, Kennedy?"

"No. I'm not kidding you."

"The other night I told you... I told you that you're my girl. My future."

My mom gasps in the corner. *Great.*

"I meant that. If you're pregnant, we're going to do this together. I love the idea of you and I having kids together. I've pictured them. Hell, I've daydreamed about baby names."

I make a scoffing sound and start to cross my arms over my chest, but then I see the silver spike through my hand. I turn my head away from it. "Ernie, you're so full of it."

"Steve is one."

I let out a laugh. "Steve?"

"Yeah, for Steve Jobs and Steve Wozniak."

"You want to name our children after nerds?"

"What? Do you want to name them after presidents?" He turns to my mom. "No offense, Mrs. Corcoran."

"None taken," she says, chuckling.

"For a girl, I thought of Tina."

"Tina?"

"For Tina Fey."

"Wait! She's not a computer nerd."

"No, but she's a genius."

"True. Very true." He's made a point there. I look over at Mom who's smiling from ear to ear. Next, I look up at Ernie. He's absently running his fingers over my good hand.

He looks up and smiles at me. "You may not be ready for this with me, but I am. I hope you're pregnant."

I hear a noise in the corner and turn my head. Mom's got tears running down her cheeks, and a tiny hiccup escapes her lips. "So happy," she squeaks.

"Mom, let's not tell anyone, okay?" I look up at Ernie. "You too. I want to know for sure, one way or the other, before we tell anyone."

"Agreed," says my mom.

"Agreed." Ernie leans down and looks at me closely. Whispering, he says, "This may scare you, Kennedy, but I'm going to say it anyway. I'm in love with you."

My mom lets out a wail in the corner, sobbing her eyes out. I roll mine. "Time will tell if that's true, Ernie. Time will tell."

He leans in and kisses my lips. "I don't give a fuck about time, Kennedy. I'm not going anywhere."

# 24

# NURSE ERNIE

## ERNIE

Her mom has offered to stay with her at her house, but I told her I was on the case. "Okay, but I can stay with her until you get your car. Plus, I'll be here tomorrow so you can go to work. How does that sound?"

"Good. Thanks, Mrs. C."

After Kennedy's released, Dad drives us both to her place. I carry Kennedy into her house and set her up on her bed. I bring her a bottle of water from her fridge and set the antibiotics and pain meds we picked up from the pharmacy next to the water. "I'm going to get my car. Your dad and brother are getting your truck and bringing it here. I'll stop and pick up something for dinner, but I'll be back in no time. Okay?"

"Uh-huh," she says, drooling a little bit. The pain meds they put her on have knocked her out. I had to carry her from the car because she was so out of it.

I pat her mom on her shoulder and run out the door. My dad's waiting for me in his pickup. "Take me to my car first. Then I'll stop at the store on the way back to her place."

"While you do that, I'll run over to your place and pack you a bag. You're going to need a change of clothes."

With Dad's help, I'm back at Kennedy's in less than an hour. I've got my arms loaded down with groceries and food from several different fast food places. I have no idea what she's going to be hungry for, so I erred on the side of caution and chose three different types. I've got macaroni and cheese, chicken, and burgers and fries.

When I walk into Kennedy's bedroom, I see she's in the same spot as she was when I left. "I should have warned you, Kennedy doesn't do well on pain medications," Jo Corcoran says, standing up from the chair in the living room.

"Has she been hurt before?" How many times has she needed them?

"Oh, um, after a procedure once."

Vague. "Okay. I'll be sure to keep a close eye on her. Should I worry?"

"No, but I'd only give her half of what the bottle recommends. It's too much for her little body to take the entire dose."

After Kennedy's mom leaves, I grab some sweats and a tee that Dad picked up for me and jump in the shower. He packed me a sizeable suitcase full of clothes and some other stuff. There are even video games stuck in and around my junk. I doubt I'll have time to play games. Taking care of Kennedy is my first priority.

After showering, I check on her. She's still passed out. I hold my hand over her nose to make sure she's still breathing. "How long are you supposed to sleep, kitten?" I run my fingers through her hair, and she lets out a soft sigh. "Good to know you're still breathing."

I make myself a plate with selections from each of the fast food places. I bought enough food for an army, so there's still plenty for her when she wakes up. I sit on her sofa, grabbing her remote. I flip on her television and check to see what kind of shit she records.

Scrolling through the list, I'm a little surprised. She's got a little bit of everything from home building and decorating shows to *Game of Thrones*. She must love car auction shows because she's got several things recorded. She's got sports, movies, comedies, and classics. I don't even need to watch live television with these choices, but I do anyway. If I'm going to watch sports; I want to see it in real-time.

Flipping around, I find the tail end of a Cubbies game. My team is up six to three in the top of the eighth. I slide down, so I'm lying lengthwise on her sofa. It's long enough for me to stretch out, and it's comfortable. In no time, I'm dozing myself. I'm awoken by a crashing sound. I jump up and race into her bedroom in time to see Kennedy's sitting on her ass, legs spread out in front of her, her back against the side of her bed. "I fell." She sticks that full bottom lip out in a pout.

"You okay, princess?"

Sighing, she says, "I love it when you call me princess, Ernie."

I lean over and put my hands beneath her armpits to lift her up. As we go up, I reply, "Yeah? Well, I love it when you call me baby."

She sucks in a gasp of air. "You do?"

"I do." I get her up high enough to set her back onto the bed. When she starts to slide off again, I wrap my arms around her and gently lay her back onto the bed.

"Well, I love calling you that. Do you know why?" She's whispering in my ear now.

"Why?"

"Because you're my sweet baby, Ernie. I adore you."

I'm taken aback by that. I love it, but it surprises the fuck out of me. "I adore you too."

I blink a few times because I see tears start to slide right out of her. "Kennedy? Why are you crying?"

"Because y-you said you adored me."

"I do. I love you."

Her little tears turn to a full-on bawling fit. "I like you too. I've liked you since forever."

*Like?* "Since forever? That's a long time, angel."

"Angel? I love that. You called me angel."

"That's because you're mine."

Her tears stop so fast I shake my head a couple of times to be sure I'm not seeing things. Her voice turns from sad to sexy. Her eyes change from brown to yellow in seconds. "And you're mine."

From out of nowhere, her little hand is down inside my sweatpants, and she's rubbing her palm up and down my shaft. I'm concentrating on not getting hard. I will *not* seduce a woman who is obviously intoxicated—drunk on pain meds. Now I think I get what her mom was saying. She gets a little wacko on the stuff.

I can't help it, though. My dick hardens from her ministrations. I take hold of her wrist and pull her hand out of my sweats. "Kennedy, you need to eat something and get some rest."

"Ernie," she whines, "I only want to eat you."

Fuck! Not right now. "You need to eat food. Later you can eat me, okay, honey?"

"Honey? You called me honey?" I stare at her as tears roll down her cheeks again.

Jesus. This is an emotional roller coaster we're dealing with here. I lay beside her on her bed and wrap my arms around her. "Shh, Kennedy. Everything's going to be okay. I've got you."

I wait for a laugh or a cry or for something sexy to come out of her mouth, but all I get is a snore. She's out again. *Thank fuck.* This nursing shit is hard work.

# 25

# IT ONLY HURTS WHEN I BREATHE

## KENNEDY

I wake myself up moaning in pain. Everything hurts—my head, arms, legs, ass, and back. Everything. Even breathing.

"Kennedy?"

I'm hearing voices now. This isn't good. I must have some sort of brain injury.

"Kennedy, sweetie?"

I slowly open my eyes to see a bright light piercing my brain. "Oh, God. I died. I see the light."

The voice giggles. "No, honey. You're alive. You need to wake up and take your medicine now. You need to eat something too."

"Not hungry," I groan. The thought of food is making me sick. I roll over to my side quickly when I realize I may actually get sick.

"Come on. Sit up and sip this water."

"Mom," I whine.

"Up, up, up, kiddo."

I roll onto my back and blink up at my ceiling. "How long have I been home?"

"You came home yesterday evening."

"Should I even ask what happened last night?" I know I react badly to some medicines.

"I'm not sure how you were in the night."

I sit up a little too fast. "Huh? Why wouldn't you know about last night?"

"Because, silly, Ernie stayed. He took care of you."

I groan loudly and flop back onto my bed. Bad idea. That sick feeling is churning up in my belly again. "Ernie? Really?"

"He insisted. He's your *future*, sweetie. He's your fella."

"My *f-fella*?" I snort out a laugh. "Mom, this isn't the 50s."

"You know what I mean. Now, sit up and take your pills. I want you to eat this toast with it. It'll settle your stomach."

"Yum." I sit up and take the bottle of water from her hand and toss back two pills. I don't even know what she's giving me. Maybe it's cyanide. I *hope* it's cyanide. "So, you're staying with me now?"

"Until Ernie gets home from work."

"What? He's coming back?"

I watch as my mom takes in a big breath. "He's your *future*. Of course, he's taking care of you."

"He's not my future!"

"Hmm, we'll see." She stands up again. "Now, eat this toast. It'll make a world of difference."

After I choke down the two bites of toast I ingested, I fall fast asleep thanks to my buddy Vicodin. When I wake up, the room is dark, and I have an intense need to use the restroom. The only light is coming from my living room. Thankfully, I don't feel as out of it as I did earlier today. I slide my body off the side of the bed, setting my feet on the ground. I push myself up to standing and start a slow trek to my en suite bathroom.

"God, I hate pain meds." They make me feel so out of control. I flip the light on in the bathroom and am blinded by the bright light. "Oh, shit." When my eyes adjust, I walk, sliding my feet across my tile until I'm in front of the toilet. I need to pee, but the urge to vomit is great too. Taking in slow, deep breaths, I choose option one. Pulling down my undies, I slowly lower myself until I'm seated. As I go, a sigh of relief escapes my mouth.

"Feel better?"

I jump so high, I nearly fall off the toilet. "Ernie!"

"What?" he says, standing in the doorway of my bathroom.

"I'm trying to pee. I need privacy."

"No can do. I don't like that you walked in here without my help. You're certainly not going to walk out without it."

"I can walk. I'm fine."

Ernie chuckles. "Whatever you say, pumpkin."

Pumpkin? When did that become one of his terms of endearment? "Pumpkin?"

"It's new. I'm trying it out. You like it?"

"No." I do, but I'm not telling him that.

"Because last night you told me how much you loved being called baby, honey, angel, and princess."

"I did not."

"Yes. You did."

"Unless you have video evidence that—"

"You also told me you adored me."

"Uh, I didn't...."

"You did." He smiles sweetly. "And I loved it."

I can tell by the softness of his expression that he did love it and it meant a lot to him. "I think you're okay, I guess."

Chuckling, he walks toward me. "Let me help you up. I don't think those meds are out of your system yet. They kind of make you a little wacky."

Groaning, I pull myself up to standing while holding onto Ernie's hand. "I've heard."

"When were you on pain meds before? Your mom said you had a procedure, but she was pretty vague about it."

I stand stock-still and stare at Ernie. "*That?* I don't talk about *that*." I pull away from him so I can reach down for my undies. Ernie beats me to it. Together we slide them up the rest of the way. I'd love to shower, but I'm too tired now. The walk to the bathroom took it out of me.

"You want to go back to bed or into the living room? I can get you set up out there if you'd like a change of scenery."

"Living room, please. I need to sit up for a while."

Ernie holds my good hand as he leads me into my living room where he's made a bed on my sofa. He pulls off the sheet and replaces it with a clean one. Plumping the pillows, he leads me to his spot on the couch. When I'm seated, I lean back as he lays a soft blanket on top of my lap.

"Now, what would you like to eat? Does anything sound good?"

"No, nothing sounds good." I shake my head.

"What about a little dish of macaroni and cheese?"

Okay, that could work. "I'll try that. No promises. I'm still a little queasy."

Before I know it, I've got a small dish of warm and gooey noodles and cheese. I dip my spoon in and take a little bite. "Good." It's warm and comforting. I eat several bites, and I'm done.

Ernie takes it from me and hands me a bottle of water. "Drink some water. You need to hydrate. I've got some Gatorade too if you'd rather."

"Water's fine."

He stares at me as I sip my water then he turns and leaves the room. I can't help watching his tight rear end as he exits. Leaning in the direction he just walked, I can hear him in the kitchen. It sounds like he's cleaning up. A few minutes pass, and he returns with a bottle of soda. He heads to my armchair, but I pat the seat next to me. "Sit with me."

He gives me a bright smile as he sits next to me, placing his arm behind me. When I feel his fingers run through my hair, I lean back and then let my head fall to his shoulder. He plays with my hair as we watch the evening news like a couple of old married folks. I hate to say it, but it's nice. I've never been in a relationship that wasn't based only on sex after.... Well, not for a long time anyway.

I look over and up at Ernie's face. "This is nice." I sound a little too surprised.

He lowers his head so he can look at me. "It is. It's very nice."

"Thanks for taking care of me."

"My pleasure. I've enjoyed most of it."

I laugh, surprised. "Most of it? Which parts didn't you enjoy?"

"That part where you cried one minute, then you had your hands down the front of my pants the next, and then you cried again right after that."

"Uh, you're crazy. I did no such thing."

"Did so."

"Wow, that's mature. '*Did so*,'" I mimicked.

He chuckles. "Go ahead and deny it. I'm glad I was here to witness it."

"What? Why?"

"Because now I know something new about you. I know you should never take pain meds unless I'm here with you. You're a menace to society on that shit."

"Ha, ha. Very funny."

"It was. But I loved taking care of you, angel."

"Are you teasing now?"

He uses his fingers to pull my chin over to face his. "Hell no,

I'm not teasing, Kennedy. For the first time in my life, I want to take care of someone other than myself, and I've never been this happy, ever."

"Oh." I stare into his eyes. "Okay, Ernie."

He leans down and kisses my lips softly. "My pleasure, pumpkin."

I snort at the new term of endearment and return to watching the TV. I fall asleep lying against his shoulder, his arm wrapped around me. Happy.

# 26

## SOFT

ERNIE

When I can't fight sleep any longer, I carry my girl back to her bed. I lay her on top of the sheet and slide her comforter over her. "Ernie?" she says sleepily.

"Yeah?"

"Stay with me."

"What about your hand? I don't want to accidentally bump it."

"It's fine. Sleep with me."

How can I refuse her? That's just it, I can't. I pull off my tee and sweats, leaving only my underwear. I slide in behind her and get as close as she'll let me. With my front pressed to her backside, I bring my arm over, sliding it beneath hers. I lay my palm on her stomach and scoot even closer. I release a happy sigh. She's so damn soft. Her skin is silky, sure, but her body, with all its roundness, is lush. Pressing against her feels like heaven.

"Ernie?"

My thoughts are interrupted by her sleepy voice. "Yeah?"

"Did you go get tested?"

"Yeah. Friday."

"Did you get results yet?"

"No. Tomorrow or the next day. I'll let you know as soon as I get them. Okay?" Tomorrow or the next day, I'll get all of the results back. I'm crossing my fingers it all works out—for everyone.

"Okay," she says as she dozes off to sleep.

I'm startled awake by someone kissing me. I look down and see Kennedy kissing my neck. She's snuggled into me with her hand running over my chest and one leg over mine. Did I mention I've got a hard-on the size of Texas? "Uh, Kennedy?"

"Mmm-hmm," she says into my skin.

"Whatcha doing, sweetheart?"

She looks up at me. "I woke up and felt like kissing you." She shrugs. "Actually," she says, sliding her little hand down my stomach right into my briefs, "I feel like doing more than kissing."

She grips me as she slides her hand up my shaft, causing my hips to jump off the bed. "You're still recovering. W-We shouldn't."

"I'm fine. My right hand doesn't hurt." She raises her eyebrows up and down.

I take hold of her wrist and pull it out of my boxers, reluctantly. "It's a bad idea."

"Ernie?"

"Yeah?"

"I need you. I'm all wet and achy down there." She points to herself.

"You are? Well, I can't have my girl all achy and needy. Is it right here?" I slide my own hand down into her panties. She's dripping.

"Yeah," she squeaks. Her squeak turns into a moan when I run my fingers through her. As I slide two fingers into her center, she rolls to her back and opens her legs for me. "Oh, fuck. Don't stop, Ernie."

But I stop. I reach over to her nightstand and open the drawer. Grasping a foil packet, I tear it open, push my briefs down, and roll it down my shaft.

"I thought you wanted to get me pregnant?" She smirks.

"I do. But not until I get my clean bill of health from my doctor."

Her face changes from a smirk to a small smile. "Thanks, Ernie."

"Don't thank me yet." I line myself up to her and thrust in all the way at once. We both moan loudly. "Now, you can thank me."

She giggles and slaps my arm. "Thank you, oh man with great big cock."

I chuckle too as I slide out. Thrusting in hard again I croak, "You're welcome, oh woman with a tiny vagina."

Kennedy throws her head back and begins to cackle. Catching her breath, she adds, "God, sex with you is fun, Ernie."

I stop moving. "Sex with me is *funny*?" I think I'm a little offended.

"No," she whispers. "Sex with you is hot and good, but it's also fun. You're the best sex I've ever had."

"I am?"

"You are. Ernie Flynn, you're number one."

We both laugh at that, and I spend the next little while making my girl less achy and no longer needy. "I love you, Kennedy."

"I think I might be able to love you too—in time."

It's my turn to laugh. I throw my head back and then look down at her. "Jesus, could you have said that in fewer words?

Why not just say, "Well, I guess it'd be possible to finally see if I could maybe feel enough for you to love you."

Peals of laughter flow from my girl. Her body is shaking she's laughing so hard. I'm having a hard time concentrating on the fucking part of the evening because when she laughs, I laugh. "God, Ernie. I do like you. You're fucking hilarious."

"You like me?" I plunge into her hard.

She moans for me. "No, that's not all. But I can't focus on serious now. Make me come."

"Yes, ma'am." I do as I'm told. Twice.

# 27

# BACK TO WORK

## KENNEDY

By Thursday, I'm feeling good enough to get back to work. Donal has been covering for me while I recover, so when I get to the site, he's already getting organized for the day. "Hey," I say as I enter my trailer.

"Hey, Kenny. You feel up to working?"

I hold up my bandaged hand and nod. "It's only a flesh wound."

Donal chuckles. "I haven't seen that movie in years."

"Monty Python. Always a classic."

"Indeed."

"So, where are we? What'd I miss?"

"Well," he says, putting his hands on his narrow hips, "I let Tim go."

"What! No!" I shout a little too loud.

"Kenny, he's a liability."

"I want him back here today!" I say, pointing to the ground. "I'm going to make that kid the best fucking... uh, damn worker you've ever had, Donal."

"He shot you with a nail gun, Kenny."

"It was an accident."

"He's a menace." Donal smirks.

"He's *my* menace. I want him back. You need to call him, though."

"Why me?"

"Because you're the real boss."

"You call him. Tell him you got him a second chance. You know, make him see you went out on a limb for him."

"Did I? Go out on a limb?"

"Sort of, but this is your jobsite. It's your call."

"Thanks, Donal."

"So, did Ernie get his results back yet?"

I gasp. Ernie has a big mouth. "Ernie told you?"

"He said he's waiting to see if he's a match."

"A match?"

"Bone marrow. Uh, didn't he tell you about that?"

I shake my head. "What bone marrow test? Is he sick?" Oh, God. He can't be sick.

"No. I shouldn't tell you since he seems to be keeping this close to his vest. But a little girl he knows has leukemia. She needs a bone marrow transplant, and they haven't been able to find a donor. Ernie is getting tested to see if he's a match."

I feel the burn of tears behind my eyes. My nose starts to tickle for the same reason. What a kind and thoughtful thing for him to do. "Who's the little girl? Is she a friend's daughter or something?" It's got to be someone he knows, right?

"He met her in the waiting room at the clinic. He said she's a 'beautiful little girl and the bravest person he ever met.'"

A tear slides down my cheek. I try to stop it, but it's not possible. "Wow, Donal. I had no idea."

"I guess he wanted to wait until he knew if he was a match before he said anything." He shrugs.

But now I know, and learning this about Ernie changes

everything. Because it's right now, right this minute, that I know for a fact that Ernie Flynn is *mine*.

"Okay, I'm sticking around today and tomorrow. You're on light duty. There's plenty of paperwork and phone calls you can make today. Sound good?"

"Sure." I sniffle a little. "I'll, uh, call Timmy first."

Donal nods and leaves the trailer.

I pick up the phone and dial. "Timmy?"

"Kenny?"

"Get your ass to work. You're late!" I shout but smile as I do it.

"Donal, he—"

"Who's your boss, Timmy?"

"Y-You, Kenny."

"That's right. Now get your ass to work. And, Timmy?"

"Yeah?" he says with a smile in his voice.

"If you fuck up one more time, I'm gonna shove a hammer so far up your ass. You get me?"

"Yeah! Thanks, Kenny! I'll be there in a minute."

I hang up feeling pretty damn good about that. When my stomach does a little flip, I realize I haven't had my coffee. "Caffeine. I need my fix."

I pull out a pod thing and pour the water into my little one-cup maker. As it brews, the scent wafts up into the air and into my nose. "Ooh, that smells terrible." I usually love the smell of coffee. Not only does it smell terrible, it's also making me feel sick.

Blame those frigging meds I was taking, they screw with me, and the fact I haven't eaten much in days. Maybe I'm hungry. I step out of the trailer in search of my cooler. I get about three steps when nausea overtakes me. I race to a trash can and throw my face in to let it go. I don't know what's worse, the puking or what's in the trash can. I yell, "Jesus! Can't anyone dump the garbage around here?"

"Kennedy?" I turn to see Ernie staring first at me then at the can. "You got sick? I told you it was too soon for you to come back to work."

I smile at him. "Light duty. I'm only working in the office today. I'll be fine."

"But I watched you puke into that disgusting can. You should be home."

"I'm fine," I say, sounding irritated. "I'm fine."

He steps closer to me. His hand reaches out, but he quickly brings it back down to his side. "Doctor's office called. They want to see me. Can I go over there during my lunch?"

"Uh, oh, sure." I wonder if this is about the bone marrow. "You take as long as you need."

"Okay. Thanks. I'll check on you later. Can I get you anything? Water?"

"Water sounds good. Thanks."

I walk back into the trailer and shut the door. Moments later, there's a knock. "Come in."

Ernie steps in holding several items. "I brought you water, a banana, and a donut from Dave."

"Ah, that's nice. Thanks."

"No problem."

As he turns to leave, I ask, "Ernie? Can I go to your doctor's appointment with you? You know, for the results."

"Uh, if you want to. Sure."

"Great. I'll meet you in the parking lot at noon. Sound good?"

"Yep. Sounds good."

28

———

## SECRETS

ERNIE

When I get to my car, Kennedy is leaning on it. "Ready?" she asks. "Wait! Should we take separate cars? I don't want anyone to see...."

"Kennedy, everyone knows."

"They do?"

"Uh, yeah. They figured it out all by themselves before Timmy shot you, but when it happened, they yelled for me to get to you. Plus, they know I stayed with you. They all know."

I watch her shoulders slump. "That's going to be a problem."

"No, it's not. If you haven't noticed anything by now, you won't. They knew I had a thing for you right away. They, uh, support us."

"They do?" She's staring at me with those big amber eyes and sighs. "Okay. Let's ride together." She slides into my car, and I get behind the wheel. As I put it into drive, she places her hand on mine. "I know about the bone marrow test."

"Jesus," I grumble. "My dad.... None of the Flynns can keep a damn secret."

"I'm glad he told me. I'm proud of you."

"What if I'm not a match?"

"I'm still proud of you. Plus, it told me something I didn't know about you."

"Oh yeah? What's that?"

She places her hand over my heart. "That your heart's big enough."

"Big enough? For what?"

I see her face blush to a beautiful pink shade. When she smiles, I feel warm inside. "It's big enough for me. I require lots of heart."

I place my hand on top of hers. "You've got *all* of mine, Kennedy."

"Wow! That's...." She pauses. "That's the sweetest thing anyone has ever said to me, Ernie Flynn. I'm speechless."

"Speechless? That won't last," I say, chuckling. I pull out into traffic, and we're on our way.

"Uh, since I know your secret, I'll tell you mine," she adds, shyly.

"You've got a secret?" I look over at her. I know I look concerned.

"The summer before I went to college, I met someone."

I nod. I'm not sure I like where this is going.

"He was older than me by a few years. He'd already graduated from college. I thought he was the most amazing man I'd ever met."

More nods, but I feel my face getting scrunched up. I already hate the guy.

"We spent every single day together. I fell hard for him— head over heels. He was my, um, my first. He said he loved me." She stops talking for a minute to gather herself. I slide my hand over and gently place it on top of her injured one.

Clearing her throat, she continues, "When I got preg-nant...." She sucks in more air and starts over. "When I got pregnant, I thought we'd get married. You know, live happily ever after." She scoffs. "That was a joke, because the minute I told him, he was literally out the door."

"That fucker!" I shout. "Who is he? I want to kick his fucking ass."

She smiles over at me. "It doesn't matter. He's a nobody. Less than a nobody."

"What happened? Did you give the baby up for adoption?"

"There were, um, complications."

"Complications?"

"It was what they call an ectopic pregnancy, or another name for it is a tubal pregnancy."

"What does that mean?"

"The baby wasn't growing in my uterus. It was growing in my fallopian tube. I had to have it removed. The baby wouldn't have survived long like that."

"Kennedy," I whisper, "I'm so sorry."

"Me too. My mom is the only other person who knows about it. Dad and my brothers would have drawn and quartered the guy for knocking me up. If they knew about the rest, I think they would have seriously killed him."

"Who was it? Do I know him?"

She shrugs. "I have no idea. He's still around. I see him every once in a while. He's married now and has a couple kids. I don't care about him. I thought I loved him, but I was mistaken. He didn't have enough heart, Ernie. Hell, he had *no* heart."

For the rest of the ride, I hold her hand. We don't talk or listen to the radio. We drive. When we arrive at the clinic, I walk around to help her out of the car. I know she's not feeling great. I wish she'd stayed home, but my girl's so damn stubborn.

---

# 29

# GETTING RESULTS

## ERNIE

When I check in with Cruella, the receptionist, she's actually nice to me. "Oh, Ernie! It's great to see you!" she says in a chipper voice. It's over-the-top squeaky and a little unnerving.

"Uh, good to see you too."

"Have a seat. The doctor will be *right* with you."

I grab the seat next to Kennedy, taking her hand in mine again, absently running my fingers on her hand. I hear her sigh.

"It's going to be okay," I say reassuringly.

"Oh, I know. This week's been overwhelming."

"I...." As I'm about to speak, I look up as the door opens. "Dad?"

"Hey, son. I thought I'd come and lend my support. I see you already have some." He squeezes Kennedy's shoulder gently.

"Thanks, Dad. I am pretty nervous. I'm glad you're here."

"I'll sit in the waiting room while you get the results." He picks up a sports magazine and starts to leaf through it. When the door opens again, I look up to see Penny Boggs.

I stand up and walk to her. "Penny? How's—"

I don't get the rest out when a cute little pixie runs right into my legs. "Ewnie!"

"Hey there, squirt." I kneel in front of her. I tap her little upturned nose that's poking out above her pink mask. "How is it you always know when I need Claire Bear?"

She's clutching onto her bear with both arms. "I'm smawt!"

"You are smart. You're the smartest, bravest little munchkin I've ever met."

Ashley beams. I stand up again. "Penny, let me introduce you to my family." My dad stands and approaches. "This is my dad, Donal Flynn. Dad, Penny Boggs."

Dad reaches his hand out slowly and waits for Penny to do the same. It's like slo-mo. "It's a pleasure," says my dad in a weird voice.

"Me too," Penny whispers.

I ignore them and keep going. "Ashley and Penny, this is my girlfriend, Kennedy."

Kennedy looks a little surprised by the introduction. We haven't labeled us yet, so I took care of that.

"You're pwetty," says Ashley with awe in her little voice.

"So are you, Ashley." Kennedy bends down to her new friend.

"What happened to your hand?" Ashley asks, concerned.

"Oh, I hurt it at work. It's getting better all the time."

"Hewe," she says, shoving Claire Bear into Kennedy's arms. "Claiwe Beaw will make you feew bettew."

"Wow, thanks so much." Kennedy gives the bear a big squeeze. "You're right! I feel better already!"

I turn to say more to Penny, but she and Dad are talking and still holding hands. Weird. Before I can figure that out, my name is called. I take Kennedy's hand and pull her along with me. "Back in a second," I say to Dad.

We're led into Dr. Merkle's office instead of an examination room. His nurse has us sit in the two chairs in front of his desk. "He'll be with you in a minute. He's finishing up with a patient."

When she shuts the door, I look at Kennedy. "I'm nervous."

Squeezing my hand, she says, "It'll be okay. No matter what."

When Dr. Merkle finally enters, I'm about ready to vomit I'm so nervous. But he doesn't waste time. I introduce Kennedy to my doctor and then he spills the news, "You're clean. There's nothing in any of the tests that concern me in the least."

I let out a whoosh of air I've been holding and look over at Kennedy. She's smiling from ear to ear. "Good news." She winks.

"*Great* news. What about...?"

"If it's all right with you, I'd like to call in Mrs. Boggs. I'd also like to speak with Ernie and Penny privately, if that's okay, Kennedy."

"Oh, of course."

I watch Kennedy step out of the room. A few minutes later, Penny steps in, confused. I guess she didn't know about any of this. "Mrs. Boggs, thank you for coming in today."

"What's this about?"

"Mr. Flynn asked me to take a sample to see if he was a bone marrow match for Ashley."

"You did?" Her eyes are twice their normal size, and her mouth is agape.

"Yeah."

She turns back to the doctor. I can tell from here she's holding her breath.

"After running the HLA, or human leukocyte antigen test, on Ernie, here, we've determined that he's an eight of eight match for Ashley."

I have no idea what he said. I heard the word match, and

then I heard Penny. I've never heard such a sound before in my life—it was a choking sound. I look over at her and see her face pressed into her hands and tears are all over the place. I look back up at Dr. Merkle and see a huge smile on his face. The conflicting emotions in the room are confusing me. "So? Am I a match?"

"Oh, God, you are!" Penny says as she throws herself into my arms. "Thank you, Ernie. I... thank you. You're our angel. Thank you." She sobs all over me.

I bring my arms up and around her to hold her into place. I let her cry her happy tears. "I'm glad I could help. She's a special little girl."

"She is. Her dad... Kent."

I wait for the rest. I want to know about that asshole.

"He died in Iraq when she was a baby. It's just been the two of us."

Okay. *Not* an asshole. *Hero* is a much better word for him.

Penny continues, "My parents and Kent's parents have been there for us. Oh my God, Ernie, this is beyond belief." Penny wipes the wetness from her face and smiles at me.

"We're not out of the woods yet, Penny," Dr. Merkle cautions her. "But I've sent everything over to Ashley's oncologist. She'll take over from here, Ernie. They'll be in touch. There are some things you need to do before they can take your marrow, but Dr. Abeal will explain everything to you in detail." He stands up and holds his hand out to me. "I'm proud of you, son."

"Thanks, Dr. Merkle."

I open the door to step out, but Penny takes hold of my arm. "I will never, ever forget what you've done for us, for Ashley. For as long as I live, you're now part of our family."

"Thanks. I feel the same about you guys too."

I lead her out to the waiting room and see Kennedy first.

She's looking at me expectantly. The second I nod and smile, I see a tear slide down her cheek. I pick up my pace so I can get to her before she loses it. I look over at my dad. He looks like someone died while Ashley is happily playing with her bear in the corner. "What's wrong?" I ask him.

Dad looks up, confused. Penny's smiling, and so am I. "I heard Penny cry out. I thought it was b-b-bad news."

"Nope. I'm a match."

A gasp from the reception desk has us all turning that way. Cruella must have overheard because she's wiping something from her face with a Kleenex. She smiles at me with her crooked smile, and I give her a weak one in return.

Penny pats my arm. "Well, I'm sure I'll see you all soon. I'll be there the day they do your procedure, Ernie."

"Sounds good. See you soon."

She walks over to my dad and gives him a hug. "You raised an amazing boy, Mr. Flynn."

"Donal. Please. Call me Donal."

Shyly, she repeats, "Donal."

Oh hell, *are they flirting?* I look down at Kennedy; she's watching them too. She turns and winks at me, and I know then. They're fucking flirting. *Finally!* Go, Dad!

30

---

## FADE TO BLACK



By the time Ernie and I get back to the jobsite, it's after two. No one says a damn word to either of us other than "hey." It's strange. For a crew of guys who are always smack-talking or teasing each other, they pretend to be completely oblivious to Ernie's and my relationship. It could also be because Donal Flynn is still hanging around. They all know better than to tease his son in front of him. Either way, it's strange. I return to my trailer and plop my tired ass in the chair. This day has been exhausting and emotional. There've been a lot of revelations today, and my brain isn't processing things as fast as I'd like. Actually, my brain hurts. My head's pounding so hard, all I want to do is sleep. "Maybe Ernie was right. I came back too soon."

I decide to do the responsible thing. I send Donal a text letting him know I'm heading home early. He replies quickly that he's got things under control. I slowly stand up from my chair and take two steps forward. I feel the ground move up toward me. That's when everything fades to black.

31

———

DEAL

ERNIE

I'm beat. I haven't slept for shit the last few nights since I've been taking care of Kennedy. I know she's tired too—not to mention the fact she's not feeling well enough to be here. My dad told me that she decided to head home early. I'm happy to hear that news. She needs to rest up.

It's not as though her injury was life threatening or anything. Honestly, I'm not sure why she's not feeling well—unless she's pregnant. But I googled that shit this morning after she threw up, and it's too soon to tell if she's got my kid inside her. It's only been, what? A week? She can get a blood test seven to ten days after we did it, or we can wait to see if she misses her period. I'm good either way.

No, her illness this morning has to do with something else. I need to keep an eye on her. I hope she's ready for me to spend another night. We haven't discussed how long I'll be staying with her, but I'm going to force the issue if she attempts to kick me out. I need to be there for her.

As for work, I've been carrying drywall today. The crew finished up installing the interior walls on the first floor, and they're working on the second floor now. They won't get that finished today, so next week will be devoted to finishing up the second and third floors.

At five o'clock, I'm ready to pass out. Dad waits for me to walk to our cars. He's dirty and dusty from working with the plumbing crew today. That's one of his favorite jobs on a site, plumbing. When we get to my car, I stop in my tracks. "Dad? I thought you said Kennedy went home."

"She did. Her text said she was heading home around two."

"Then why is her truck still here?" I point to her blue Ford F-150.

As Dad starts to provide the standard "she must have taken a cab" reason, I toss my shit down and run to the trailer. Yanking the door open, I take the two steps up in one. I look right then left and then down. "Kennedy!"

I kneel down to her and see she's on her side with her arm underneath her head; her eyes are closed. I gently touch the side of her face and then slide my fingers to her neck. She's not moving, but she's breathing and has a pulse. Dad wrenches open the door and looks inside. "What's wrong? What happened?"

"Dad? I don't know." I look back down at her. "Kennedy? Wake up, honey."

"I'll call 911. Don't move her, son. We don't know what happened."

"Hang on, her eyes are blinking."

"Ernie?" she says weakly.

"I'm here. Don't move. I'm calling 9-1-1!"

"No, not again. I fainted for a second. When I woke up, I decided to stay put and get some sleep. My entire body hurts," she says with a groan.

"Are you going to be okay if I carry you? If not, we're calling an ambulance."

"I can walk."

"No, you can't." I turn to Dad. "Can you pull your truck up closer? We need to take her to the ER."

"Sure, back in a few." Dad takes off at a jog.

"I feel like shit, Ernie. What's wrong with me?"

"I don't know, princess. I've got you. We'll figure this out."

Back in the ER, it's like déjà vu all over again. Kennedy's mom is sitting in the chair in the corner, and I'm standing next to her bed while we wait for one of the doctors to come tell us what's going on with my girl.

We don't have to wait long. A woman in a white lab coat steps into the room. "Hello, I'm Dr. Mallory. How's the patient doing?"

"I feel like crap. Everything hurts."

"Well, we ran a few tests, and we believe you're severely dehydrated, Ms. Corcoran."

"That's it? I'm dehydrated? I drink water."

"Don't underestimate the damage dehydration can cause, Kennedy. To name a few things, it can cause dizziness, nausea, fatigue, muscle aches and pains, cramps, headaches, disorientation, blurred vision, chills, and or fever, and it can affect your mood as well."

"I had no idea," whispers Kennedy.

"You're going to feel kind of crappy for a day or two. We're going to give you an IV of fluids to get you started, but then I want you to take it easy for a few days, drink plenty of liquids, eat healthy foods, and rest. Can you do that, Kennedy?"

"She can. I'll make sure of it." I take Kennedy's hand in mine, running my fingers over her palm and wrist. "Right, Kennedy?"

"Right."

"Right!" says Mrs. C from the corner.

We all laugh at her little shout as the doctor orders the IV of fluids. "Once the bag is empty, I'll release you as long as you do as I say." Dr. Mallory looks at Kennedy sternly.

"I will."

"Good. I'll be back to check on you."

"Thanks, Doctor."

"Well, that's a relief," says Jo. "You scared the bejesus out of your dad and me. You need to take more than a few days off, sweetie. You're no good to anyone if you're sick."

"She's right, babe."

"Fine," she says without any bluster. "I will. Donal will take over. It's not a big deal." She pouts.

"It isn't a big deal. You're a great boss, and you lead a tight ship, but you need to take care of yourself." I lean down and kiss her lips gently. "Okay?"

"Okay."

"So, Mrs. C., same deal as last time? You stay with her during the day while I'm at work?"

"Of course."

Kennedy says nothing. She growls from her hospital bed as the nurse comes in to administer the IV. Damn, my girl is stubborn.

# 32

# BACK TO NORMAL

## KENNEDY

God, I'm worthless and pathetic. I'm going stir-crazy having been cooped up in my house for four days. I'm going back tomorrow, even if Ernie tries to stop me. I feel 100 percent better, so I'm ready to go.

When Ernie and I get to the site on Tuesday, Donal's gone and Ed Flynn is there in his place. I like Ed. He's a good man. It's just, well, he's serious. Okay, not merely serious. The guy is *uber* serious. In a way, I feel a little sorry for Ed. He always seems sort of sad. He never smiles. He carries around a giant planner filled with a calendar, legal pad, and a calculator everywhere he goes. I'm not sure what he writes in there. Whatever it is, it's detailed. Ernie says his big brother Ed is a "stick in the mud" and "he's got a stick up his ass."

I like Ed though. He's always been kind to me, albeit not overly demonstrative. I've observed him in his natural habitat, and my guess is that Ed takes his responsibility as the big brother to two rather immature brothers and as second-in-command after Donal, to the *nth* degree. I don't mind that he's at the site today. He knows what he's doing, even though he prefers to work on the residential projects more than he does the commercial side of the business.

His renovations of the more historic properties are amazing. He takes great pride in returning a home back to its former glory —something I believe in since I lovingly restored my little Craftsman bungalow myself. It took me years, though, even with the help of my family. Mom and Dad helped me buy my place. In private, Mom told me she thought it'd help take my mind off the baby and that it'd also be a great investment, and I could live there and work on it while I went to school at the University of Illinois-Chicago. Mom was right. I loved having a project to work on even though it took me years to finish.

After talking with Ed and giving my assurance that I'm all better, he decides to head out to his site instead of micro-managing mine. The guys are happy to see me. The first one to approach me is Tim. I haven't spoken to him since I hired him back.

"How's it going? Kill anyone today?" I tease.

"No," he says, lowering his head. "I'm being careful and listening to Dave. I, uh, I'm sorry about that, Kennedy."

"I know, Tim. We're good. Pay attention and be safe. Got it?"

"Got it."

At lunch, Ernie and I sit next to each other over by the one and only tree left on the site. "Ethan and Claire want us to come over for game night tonight," Ernie says hesitantly.

"Game night?"

"Yeah, they play board games or some shit. It's a front though. They want to see you and me together. They don't believe the rumors."

I giggle as I sip my water. "It sounds fun. You said Claire's cool, right?"

"Yeah, she's very cool. But my brother...."

I laugh again. Ethan Flynn is a great guy. I don't get Ernie's remarks about his little brother. "Yeah, let's do it."

"Claire called it a double date," Ernie says shyly.

"I suppose it is."

"I haven't even taken you out on a *real* date, just the two of us."

"We've been busy."

Ernie rolls his eyes. "You can say that again."

"We've been busy."

"Ha, fucking ha." Ernie leans over then and kisses me quickly on the mouth. "I want to take you out, Kennedy. Somewhere nice. Will you go out with me?"

Ernie notices me looking around the place to be sure no one saw him kiss me and says, "Give it a rest. They all know. I'm not going to attack you in public, but I'm also not going to pretend you're not my woman. Get used to it. So? Date?"

"Of course. I'd love to go on a date with you. Tell me when." I sip my water. "You know, you're getting awfully alpha male on me, Ernie." I lean over to whisper in his ear. "Better watch out. Bad boys get spanked."

I watch Ernie's eyes double in size as a smirk appears on his lips. "Only if you use that little hand of yours. No more metal rulers."

"Absolutely. Keep up that sassy attitude, I may have to spank you tonight. Uh, after game night."

"Great. Now that's all I'm going to think about all day and night."

I smile and stand. "Get back to work, Cherry."

"I'm not Cherry anymore! You've hired two guys since me. Let that go."

I shake my finger in front of his face and quietly say, "Now you really are a very naughty boy. No back talk, Ernest."

Chuckling, Ernie shakes his head and stuffs the last bite of the sub I made him this morning into his mouth. Swallowing, he mutters, "Noted."

# 33

# GAME NIGHT

## KENNEDY

"You sure you want to do this?" Ernie looks down at me. The plate he's holding filled with cheese and crackers is shaking slightly.

*Aww, Ernie's nervous.*

"I'm sure. This is an excellent way to get to know Claire."

Ernie raises his fist and knocks on Ethan and Claire's door. When we hear a female voice say, "It's open," he turns the knob and we enter.

Ernie lets me walk in first. A pretty woman with deep purple hair greets me. "Kennedy?"

"Yes. Claire?"

She wraps her arms around me and squeezes me tightly. "It's so great to meet you!"

"Same here. Although, I have to admit, I'm at a disadvantage. Ernie has been pretty stingy with his information about you and Ethan."

"That's because he's a dick," shouts Ethan Flynn from the kitchen.

"He's not a dick!" shouts Claire. "You're jealous, Ethan. He landed himself a hottie."

Walking my way, Ethan defends, "Hey, I landed a hottie too!"

I look up at Ernie and notice that he's standing stiffly beside me. "We brought some cheese and crackers," I say, changing the subject.

"Ooh, great!" says Claire taking the plate from me. "This will go great with my dip." I follow Claire into the kitchen. As soon as we cross the kitchen threshold, Claire sets the plate down, then turns back to me quickly and wraps her arms around me again. "I'm so happy for you guys. Ernie seems so happy. I've never seen him this happy, and I've known him six years, Kennedy."

"Uh...."

"I mean, he never stops talking about you. And let me say, that's something because Ernie spent the last six years only talking about himself." She snorts out a laugh and squeezes me again. "God, I'm so happy for you both."

When we separate, I see shiny tears on Claire's face. "Wow. You are happy."

"Oh yeah. I'm so glad you're not a skinny, blonde bimbo."

"Uh...." Is that a compliment? Is that what he usually dates? I never gave that any thought. He likes thin blondes? I couldn't be further from that if I tried. "Has he dated a lot of blondes?"

"Oh, *tons!*" she emphasizes "tons." "I could tell you some stories."

"Uh, well, okay." Honestly, I have zero interest in hearing about his past women. I'm too busy wondering what the hell he's doing with me. I mean, I know the kind of women he slept with before—some of them were friends of mine. My eyelashes flutter quickly while I try to picture them. I suck in a quick breath when I realize Claire's right. They're all blonde, thin, and gorgeous.

*What the hell was I thinking? I've been deluding myself.*

Claire stops and stares at my face. "Oh, shit. I'm so sorry. What am I talking about? None of those women stayed longer than one night. I've never, and I mean never, seen him like this. You're the real deal. Please don't let my stupid jokes make you doubt his feelings. I'm his best friend, Kennedy. I know he's hopelessly in love with you."

"Okay." I smile. I need to let all this information roll around in my head for a little while. Changing the subject, I ask, "So, what games are we going to play?"

TRIVIAL PURSUIT WAS CREATED by the Devil. Why I ever agreed to do one of those battle of the sexes deals, I'll never know because Ernie Flynn is s-m-a-r-t. I think he's remembered everything he's ever watched, read, or heard over the span of his entire life. I'm pretty sure Ethan knew this about Ernie. But why Claire didn't plan better... I have no idea.

"We win," says Ernie smugly.

"You cheated!" I shout and laugh at the same time.

"You've landed yourself a genius, girl. Get used to it. Next time, don't volunteer to be on another team," Ernie says, looking cocky.

I raise my arms up and down like I'm praising him. "You're a god at Trivial Pursuit. I'll never be on the opposing team ever again."

"Hey, change of subject here, but did you go get measured for your tux, Ern?" asks Claire.

Ernie stares at Claire and blinks like he has no idea what she's talking about.

"Ernie!" Claire whines. "The wedding is in less than two weeks, and you need to go get measured. There's a place like a block from your apartment. I picked it for that reason."

"Sorry, I'll do it this week."

"No!" Standing, Claire shoves her hands onto her hips. "Tomorrow!"

"I'll get there. Don't worry about it," Ernie says, waving her off.

I'd heard the Flynns talking about Claire and Ethan's wedding, but I didn't realize it was so soon. "I'll be sure he goes." I squeeze Ernie's thigh under the table and look him up and down. "You'll look hot in a tux."

"I'll go tomorrow," Ernie says quickly.

Claire laughs. "Damn. I should have gotten you involved a long time ago." Taking a sip of her beer, she adds, "Which reminds me—"

"Uh-oh. Better run, Kennedy," teases Ethan.

Ignoring him, Claire continues. "Ed is walking with my friend Scarlett since he's Ethan's best man. Ernie, my *Dude of Honor*, has no one to walk with, so would you consider doing that for me?"

"Uh, but we just met."

"And I already feel like we're going to be great friends. It's nothing fancy. Donal is performing the ceremony. The actual wedding is small. The reception is going to be a little bigger. All you need is a black cocktail dress." She smiles at me adding, "Please?"

"Well, I do already have a black dress."

"You're not wearing that!" says Ernie angrily.

"Uh, yeah, I am." That was an expensive dress. I owe it to myself to wear it often.

"No. You. Are. Not!"

"And why can't I wear that dress?" It's my turn to stand with hands on hips.

"Because, Kennedy, you wore that on a date with another

fucking guy. I'll buy you a new dress. Fuck, I'll buy you ten if you promise to burn that fucking dress."

I blink at him and see how upset he is about that. "Okay," I whisper, "I didn't realize that upset you so much. I'll get a new dress." I turn to Claire. "I'd love to walk down the aisle with Ernie."

I sit back down and see a gleam in Claire's eye. I turn to Ethan and see a smirk and then to Ernie who's smiling at me. "You want to walk down the aisle with me?" he asks.

I don't get what the big deal is; we're going to walk down.... "Oh, I meant—"

"We know what you meant. I loved seeing Ernie's smile after you said it." Claire winks.

"Okay. What say we play Monopoly?" Ethan says rubbing his hands together like he's ready to battle and win.

Ernie groans at that. "You know I fucking hate that game. Let's play Cards Against Humanity."

I've never played that one, but I'm game. "Sounds good to me."

Claire jumps up and grabs the game. "Battle of the sexes?"

I start to say "yes" when Ernie grabs my thigh. "You're with me, babe. We're going to annihilate these two."

"Oh." I smile. "Okay. Sorry, Claire."

"No problem. Ethan, it's you and me. Let's kick their asses."

And that's what Claire and Ethan did. They kicked our asses.

# 34

## THE NEXT PHASE

### ERNIE

The ride home from my brother's place is quiet. Kennedy hasn't said a word since we left. I can't tell if she's tired or mad. I'm going to hope it's the first one because I can't remember doing anything wrong.

"You okay, Kennedy?"

"Huh?" She looks over to me. "Oh, yeah. Great."

"You aren't saying much. Did you have a good time?"

I get a smile. "I did. They're fun. I liked Claire. I can see why you've been friends for so long."

"Yeah, she's cool." Kennedy remains mute, so I ask again, "Are you sure you're okay?"

With a sigh, she does her best to reassure me. "I'm fine. Just tired."

That's true, she's tired. Today was her first day back to work after all of her health stuff. "We'll be home in a couple of minutes." *Home?* I called Kennedy's place home. Come to think of it, I haven't been to my place, except to pick up clothes and shit, for a week. It feels like we've moved on to the next phase of the relationship. I love the idea of the next phase, but does Kennedy feel the same? Now I wonder if she's tired of me staying with her. I don't want to ask though. If I ask, it'll become a *thing*. I like staying with her. It feels right, natural. I could rent my place out and start paying half the bills at her house. I know if I bring it up, I'll end up back at my place. That's how shit works with women.

"So, I've been thinking...." What the hell am I doing? I told myself I wasn't going to bring this up.

"That's dangerous." She smirks. "What were you thinking?"

"Well, I was thinking I should rent my place out and—"

"No. I'm not ready for all of that yet."

Okay. So far, she hasn't said anything about me going home.

"You don't need to stay with me, Ernie. I'm fine now. You want to stay at your place now, right?"

*Boom*, there it is. But I've still got a chance. She didn't say she wants me to go; she gave me an out.

"Do you want me to go? I like staying with you, but if you want me to go...."

"Not tonight. Stay tonight. But, yeah, this is getting pretty serious pretty fast—a little too fast for me."

I nod and stare out the window. I'd love to punch myself in the face right now. If I hadn't brought it up, I'd be in Kennedy's bed for the foreseeable future. But no! I had to ask her if she wanted me to leave. Jesus, I'm a fucking idiot!

At Kennedy's, I follow her into the bedroom. She quickly changes into one of my T-shirts and climbs into bed. I strip down to my boxers, but before I climb in, I grab a small bottle of Gatorade from the fridge. "Here, babe. Drink this."

"I drank a gallon of water at your brother's tonight."

I stare down at her with a look that I hope says, "Drink this or else."

She lets out an angry breath. "Fine. You're such a mother hen."

"Call me all the names you want, princess. As long as you drink this, I don't mind."

After she drinks, I slide into bed behind her and wrap my arm around her middle, pulling her to me. I love to spoon. Something I never thought I'd admit to myself, ever. Having Kennedy's soft form right against mine is an unbelievable feeling. "So, you're going shopping with Claire this week?"

"Yeah, that's the plan."

"I can get you out of it if you want me to."

"No. I like Claire. It'll be fun."

"Are you going out with her and Scarlett next weekend too?"

"I'm not sure about that one. Let's see how I feel."

"Sounds like a good plan." I lean over and kiss the side of her neck. "Love you, babe."

She sort of mumbles vaguely in response. Kennedy hasn't said she loves me yet. I'm not sure when or if that will ever happen. I'm okay with that for now, but if it goes on for too long, I'll have to reassess. I can't *make* her love me. She's got to do that all on her own. My job is to be the best boyfriend I can be. I've got to prove to her that I'm worth loving. Keeping my arm around her, I lay my head back onto my pillow. Before long, she's snoring softly next to me, and it makes me smile. It's such a cute sound. I let my mind swirl around the notion that I need to prove that I'm worth keeping. I'll ask my dad about that. According to him, he romanced my mom right down the aisle. He'll know what to do.

# 35

# SHOP 'TIL YOU DROP

## KENNEDY

"I didn't know it was actually possible to shop until you dropped," I say, plopping my ass down onto my chair. Claire and I have been walking up and down Michigan Avenue for hours. I only worked a half day today, so I could meet Claire for, as she calls it, our big "shopping adventure." Now, it's eight o'clock at night, and we're finally sitting down for dinner.

"I know. My feet are killing me." Claire slides off the offending footwear.

"Well, those shoes are damn cute. Sometimes you've got to suffer for fashion." I snort.

"Yeah, right. I'm more of a sneaker and T-shirt kind of girl. I don't know what I was thinking wearing these strappy wedges."

"Because it goes with your dress. Converse sneakers would have ruined it."

"True. Okay, what are you going to order?"

We're at a little restaurant on Michigan called Sweetwater Tavern and Grille. Neither of us have ever been here, but the menu that's posted outside the front door looks good and not too over the top with pretentious food. I order the Philly steak with tots and a glass of water while Claire gets adventurous and orders the lobster mac 'n' cheese and white wine. My stomach does a little flip thinking about adding seafood to nature's perfect food. *Blasphemy.*

"So, are you going out with Scarlett and me on Saturday? It's my 'bachelorette' party," she says, using air quotes. "I'm not calling it that though."

"Why not?"

She snickers. "It makes Ethan nervous. He thinks I'll get so drunk I'll hook up with a stripper or something. But that's definitely not my style."

"Ernie didn't mention a bachelor party. Are they going out too?"

"Yeah, but something tells me we'll be seeing them at some point in the night. I don't think Ernie likes the idea of you doing the bachelorette thing either."

I roll my eyes. "He doesn't care."

"Uh, yeah, he does. He told me if I took you any place that had naked men or any kind of drunken debauchery, he'd hurt me." She giggles.

"Drunken debauchery? Sign me up!"

When our dinner arrives, my stomach growls angrily. "I'm starving." I bite into my sandwich. "Mm, good."

"It is. I need to remember this place. It's yum-city," says Claire as she takes another bite.

We chitchat through our meal, and then we part ways. I grab a cab home. I'm too tired to wait for a bus. When I slide out of the cab, I see my house is completely dark. Suddenly, I'm sad that Ernie's not here. He did as I asked and went back to his place. My bed was cold and lonely last night, but I refuse to call him. To be completely honest, I'd like nothing more than to snuggle up to the big guy, but this is for the best.

I slowly walk up to my door. As I dig the keys out of my pocket, I hear, "Did you have fun today?"

I shriek and jump back. "Jesus! Stop doing that! You scared the bejesus out of me, asshole."

Ernie chuckles as he wraps his arms around me from the back. "Sorry, princess. I wanted to be sure you got home safely." He leans in and kisses my neck, causing me to moan at the sensation. When he bites down, I squeak. My nipples peak immediately. "Ernie," I say breathlessly.

"You miss me?" He licks the spot he just bit.

"No." I turn in his arms and wrap mine around his neck, pulling him down for a hot kiss. I take the lead, sliding my tongue into his mouth. Ernie's hands move quickly to my ass as he pulls me up, pressing me against my front door. "You're already hard?"

"I've been hard for an hour thinking about you coming home."

"You have?" I say, kissing down his neck. I bite him the same way he bit me, which makes Ernie press his cock into me.

"I need to fuck you, Kennedy. It's been too long."

It's only been a little over a week, but it feels longer. "I need you too, Ernie."

He sets me down and picks up my dropped keys and my shopping bags. Unlocking the door, he holds it open for me to enter first. Once inside, he drops everything onto the floor and grabs me, lifting me off the ground and carrying me to my bedroom.

Setting me on the bed, he starts to strip. "Clothes off, Kennedy."

*Bossy much?* I quickly strip down to bra and panties, and he stops midstriptease to stare at me. "New panties, sweetheart?"

"Yeah. You like?"

"I like. But I'll like them even better when they're on the floor." I stand up and turn. Bending down, I slowly push my new light blue undies down my legs. I wiggle my ass as I go, and

Ernie practically snarls. "Fuck, you're so goddamn sexy, Kennedy."

As I hoped, Ernie moves right up behind me until our bodies are pressed together. His hands unhook my matching bra, and I pull it off and drop it to the floor. With one hand, he cups my left breast. With the other, he cups my sex, sliding a finger through my slit. "You're fucking drenched."

"I want you inside of me. Now, Ernie."

He places his hand on the back of my neck and gently pushes me downward. "Hands on the bed."

I place my hands on the bed, but I decide to move up. With my knees on the very edge of the bed and my face pressed down onto the mattress, I feel him slide through me. Without a word, he pushes himself into me with one thrust.

"Goddamn, Kennedy. You're so fucking tight this way."

"Uh-huh," I pant. "Move. Please."

Sliding back out, he grips my hips and thrusts, pounding into me over and over again. I do my part, pushing back as he slides inside. We've found a rhythm that's making me thrum. I feel myself squeezing him involuntarily. My orgasm comes from out of nowhere, and my grip on his cock has to hurt. "Holy...," he grunts. "So good."

"Yeah." *So good.* He's not finished. Pulling me up, so I'm kneeling now, he reaches around, cupping both of my breasts in his big hands. "I love you so fucking much, Kennedy." He comes like a rocket, shouting my name. Then I feel it. He did it again. He didn't wear a freaking condom.

"Ernie!"

"What?" His hands are still holding me upright, but I can tell he's looking down as he slides out.

"You didn't wear a damn condom again?"

"Nope."

"That's pretty fucking stupid."

"Why?"

"Because, numb nuts, I'm not on birth control. You know that. We talked about it."

"No, we talked about me getting tested. I got tested. I'm clean."

"We could have made a baby."

"I know." His big smile lights up his entire face.

I scoot up onto the bed and turn to face him. "Ernie, we're not ready for that."

"You could already be pregnant, Kennedy. We both know that."

"Getting pregnant should be a decision we make together. Yes, I should have made sure you wrapped that big boy up. From now on, you need a condom."

"Fine," he growls. I watch him walk into the bathroom.

When the door slams, I blink. "He wants to get me pregnant?"

"Yeah!" he shouts from inside the bathroom. "I want to get you pregnant."

Sliding on my sleep T-shirt, I yell my response, "It's not your decision to make, Ernie. It's mine."

He opens the door. "It's both of ours. I should have worn a condom. I'm sorry. Just know, the minute you're ready, I'll be ready." Still naked, Ernie slides into bed behind me. I feel his hand slide around my middle, and then I'm pressed into him. Sighing, I lay my head on my pillow, enjoying the warmth of his big body. I'm lucky, my guy loves to spoon. Neither of us says anything more. We both fall asleep wrapped up together.

I could get used to this.

---

# FOR THE BEST

KENNEDY

On Saturday I wake up early, feeling achy. I look over at Ernie who is still fast asleep. He hasn't gone back to his place after my day with Claire. I'm not sure I want him to go back home. I like him here. He's a fun roommate. No, I'm not talking about the sex. Well, not *just* the sex. He's easy to live with. Whatever I want to watch, we watch. Whatever I want to eat, he either makes or buys. I'm feeling like a real princess. I know he calls me "princess," but I don't need to act like one.

Hell, I've taken care of myself for years. Having someone doting on me is nice. I'll reciprocate, don't worry. There will come a time when the shoe is on the other foot, no doubt sooner than I'd like. I smile at that thought as I walk into my bathroom in search of something for my headache. When I sit down on the toilet. I catch a glimpse of the inside of my panties. The spots of blood aren't a surprise; it's that time of the month. But the tear that slides down my cheek is surprising. I wipe it away. "It's okay. It's too soon for us to get pregnant anyway." I wipe and reach down to open the cupboard beneath the sink. Grabbing a tampon, I remove my panties and toss them in the hamper. I'll grab a clean pair from the bedroom when I'm done.

My pain relief meds are in my medicine cabinet. Sifting through the bottles, I can't see the labels. My single tear from a minute ago has reproduced. "Oh, fuck." My mind starts to battle. *Reproduced? What did I expect? To get pregnant the two times we did it without a condom? Why not? It happened the first time. Yeah, but you were eighteen.* I was as fertile as a cat in heat back then.

Taking tissue from the roll, I wipe away the tears. It's not uncommon for me to get weepy at this time of the month. Ugh, that thought starts off the whole thing again. "Babe?" he says from the bed.

Oh, fucking great! He's awake. "Yeah," I say, trying to disguise my voice.

"You okay?"

"Yeah." *No.*

"Come back to bed."

I wipe my eyes one more time and saunter out of the bathroom, doing the best I can to act normal. I turn so my back is to him and slide into the bed. It's awkward, but this way he can't see my face.

His palm finds my stomach, but as he pulls me into him, I wince. Cramps. "Kennedy? What's wrong? Did I hurt you just now?"

"No." I let the tears fall now. He might as well know. "I got my period," I wail.

He uses his hand to roll me to face him. "Kennedy. It's okay. Don't cry, angel."

His sweetness makes me cry even harder. When he wraps his arms around me and holds me, I'm nearly beside myself. After a long while, my sobbing slows to a few tears. "I don't know why it upset me so much. It's too soon, right?"

"Maybe. You must have wanted it more than you thought, huh?"

"Maybe."

"We can keep trying. You know I want to. But I want you, and I to be on the same page."

"Me too. But I don't think I'm ready. If I had been pregnant this time, I wouldn't have minded, but now that I'm not, I think we need to be careful."

"All right, Kennedy." He rubs my back and kisses my forehead. "I love you."

I hum an affirmative kind of sound because I can't do it. I can't say it. It's too fucking scary.

WE SLEEP another couple of hours. I'm always extra tired when it's that time of the month. When I flutter my eyes open, Ernie's staring at me.

"You okay?"

It's then I remember this morning. A sense of sadness rushes through me, but I refuse to cry again. "Yeah. I'm fine."

"You still going out with Claire and Scarlett tonight?"

I groan. I don't want to go, but I promised. "Yeah." I guess I can drink now. *Yippee.*

He slides his hand over my cheek and into my hair. "Everything's going to be okay, princess."

When he twists his fingers around some of my curls, I close my eyes. "I love it when you play with my hair."

"You do?"

"Yeah."

He plays with it some more until he leans in to kiss me sweetly on the lips. That gentle kiss leads to touching, licking, and more kissing. He knows I'm sad and that I don't feel great, but his touches are what I needed. Gentle and kind Ernie Flynn. Who knew?

# 37

# DRUNKEN DEBAUCHERY

## ERNIE

When I finally get the call at two in the morning, I'm relieved and pissed. "Er-Ernie?" slurs my drunk-as-a-skunk girlfriend.

"Kennedy? Where are you?"

"Uh, um...." I hear her pull away from her phone. "Hey!" she shouts away from the phone. "Where the fuck am I?"

I wait patiently for her to come back on the line. "Babe?"

"Hey, Ernie. Whatcha doin'?"

"Waiting for you to call. Tell me where you are, and I'll come get you." When she giggles into the phone, I grit my teeth, doing my best to keep my anger in check. "Kennedy? Princess? Where are you?" See, I sounded sweet there. I can do this.

"Well, uh...." She sighs. "I'm at Dreamstuds."

"Dreamstuds?" *Don't get angry. Don't get mad.*

"No! Dreamboys! Yeah! That's it."

"Dreamboys?" Gritting my teeth, I squeak, "What kind of place is that?" Oh, I know the kind of place it is, and I'm going to fucking kill Claire. I put her on speakerphone and google the address. Fuck! It's over on West Ontario. It's going to take me thirty plus minutes to get there.

"It's a club full of *reeeaaallly* sexy naked guys." She snorts then giggles.

"Kennedy?"

Then, in a sexy-as-fuck voice, she adds, "Not as sexy as you are though. Ernie, you're the fucking sexiest man I've ever met in my life. I think we should institute the 'Ernie naked all day' policy forthwith!" she shouts.

*Forthwith?* "Babe? I'm coming to pick you up. I'll grab the others too and take them home."

"Oh, Ethan already came for Claire. God, Ernie. She was *waaaasted*. You should have seen her."

"Ethan didn't take you with?" Why the fuck didn't Ethan pick her up?

"Yeah, Ethan tried to get me to go with him, but I lied and told him you were on the way. I wanted to stay for pictures."

"Pictures?"

"Hell yeah! I got my picture taken with the boys. I think one of them felt me up, but whatevs." She sighs.

Gritting my teeth, I say, "Well, then Scarlett. I'll take her—"

"She already left too. She was a sport though. For a girl who doesn't like the dick, she was a lot of fun."

"So, you're there alone?" I'm trying to control my voice, so I don't start yelling into the receiver.

"No. There are other people here. Why?"

"Why? It's not safe—"

Interrupting me, she yawns. "Are you almost here? I'm tired."

I'm already in my car working my way to Milwaukee Avenue. "On my way. Sit tight. Stay inside, Kennedy." When she doesn't respond, I try again, "Kennedy?"

"Huh? What?"

"Stay. Inside."

"Oh, sure. I will. Bye-bye, sweet cheeks." She hangs up with a click. I quickly try to call her back. I'd rather have her on the phone with me, but she won't pick up.

"Goddamn it!" I'm going to kill my best friend. I hit the gas and hope to fuck I don't get stopped. Hopping onto I-90, I gun the car and get to the fucking male strip club in about twenty-five minutes. Double-parking my car, I hit the flashers and jump out onto the street. As I run to the door, I see red to my left. "Kennedy!"

She's stumbling down the sidewalk about to cross the street. "Kennedy?" I run as fast as I can to get to her. Jesus, she's wasted.

She turns to face me. "Oh, hey. What're you doing here?"

"I came to pick you up."

"Oh, you didn't need to do that." She slaps my chest. "I was going to catch a cab."

"Well, I'm here now. So, come on." I take her hand and then wrap my arm around her. In an attempt to keep myself from going crazy, I ask, "Have fun?"

"Oh my God, Ernie, the show was *soooo* good. Those guys can dance. I wish...." She pauses. "I just wish they would have gotten completely naked. But they teased us by showing us ass and no dick."

"Well, it's the law, I think."

She stops abruptly, slamming her hands on her hips. "Well, that law is bullshit!"

I chuckle. "I know. I'll make some calls about it tomorrow, okay?"

"You will?" she asks sweetly.

"I will. For you, anything." I mean that. I'd do about anything... except I won't be making any fucking phone calls about fucking male strippers. I draw the line at that.

"I l-like you so much, Ernie."

*She likes me so much?* She *likes* me? This night gets better and better.

"Ooh, wait! Look at my pictures." Kennedy reaches into her purse and pulls out two photos of herself and the men from Dreamboys. In one she's lying across the laps of three of the guys, surrounded by five others. They're all looking at her with hungry eyes. Fucking assholes. In another one, she's straddling the center guy and looking back at the camera with a smile that says it all.

I flip over one of the pictures and see writing.

*BEAUTIFUL KENNEDY. Call me. 312-697-1778. Dirk.*

*DIRK?* What kind of fucking name is Dirk? *Keep calm, Ernie. Keep calm.* But all I want to do is tear the fucking pictures into tiny shreds.

"Aren't they cute?" she asks sweetly.

"Uh-huh. Adorable. Come on, Kennedy. I'm tired. Let's get going."

"Fine! You're no fun!" She crosses her arms in front of her. "Party pooper."

"Yep, that's me. Now hop in so I can get us home."

Once I've got her buckled into the seat, I hit the blinker and ease out onto the street. I look over and see she's already passed out, clutching the pictures tightly. I should throw them away. She'll never remember them. Right?

We get to her place, I park and slide out of the car. When I open her door, she nearly falls out. I reach under her, lifting her into my arms.

"Ernie?" she says groggily.

"Yeah, princess?"

Her breath hitches, and she starts to cry. "I'm sad."

"Why?" I hope to fuck she doesn't say she's sad about leaving the Dreamboys.

"I-I'm sad I'm not pregnant."

"I know. Me too, baby."

That was the wrong thing to say because the crying intensifies. I know most of this is emotion caused by drinking too much and maybe because it's that time of the month, but she's sad nonetheless.

"Shh, it's all right. We're home. Let's get you into a shower and tucked into bed. You hungry?"

Her tears stop. "Yes! Starving!"

"I'll make you something to eat after your shower. How's that?"

She kisses my cheek. "Thanks, Ernie."

"You're welcome." *I love you.* I think it to myself. I made a promise to myself tonight—until she says it to me, I need to keep it to myself. I hope I can keep that promise.

# 38

## KILL ME NOW

### KENNEDY

Someone, please, kill me now. My head feels like someone took a hammer to it, and I haven't even opened my eyes yet. I slowly open one eye, hoping and praying wherever I'm sleeping is still dark. Nope, no such luck. The bright sunlight slices across the room straight across my face. "Oh, hell." I moan into my pillow.

"Not feeling the best?"

"No, smart-ass. I feel like double shit."

"Wow, that's bad. Here, I brought you a glass of water and a bottle of Gatorade, along with some pain reliever."

I slowly roll toward the voice. "Bless you, my son."

"Nuh-uh. No using church lingo after you spent the night at a strip club. God's not going to listen to you until you repent."

"Repent? Since when did you get all holier-than-thou?"

"You were a bad, bad girl last night, princess. You're going to be paying for that for a while."

I flop to my back. "Why? It wasn't even my idea to go. It was—"

"Whose idea was it to get their picture taken with the entire crew of Dreamdouchebags?"

"It's Dreamboys." I groan again. "Oh, hell, I did that?"

"You did. I'm afraid I've confiscated the photos."

"Good. Burn them."

"Already handled."

"Wait!" I sit up too quickly. I'm about to protest the destruction of my personal property when the overwhelming need to yack hits me. I roll off the side of the bed and stagger to the bathroom as fast as I can. Luckily, I make it to the porcelain goddess in time.

I feel Ernie's hand move my hair out of my way. He rubs my back gently until I don't think I can get sick any more. "Thanks," I say, still gagging a little bit.

"Can you stand?"

"I think so." But when I pull myself up, I sway first away from Ernie then toward him. "Oh, I'm gonna...." I turn and repeat the process. There wasn't much in my stomach, so it hurts.

I try standing again, but this time I hold onto Ernie's arm. He hands me a cold cloth, and I wipe my face with it. "Let's get you back to bed. I'll bring you a cool cloth for your head. Okay?"

"You're so good to me, Ernie."

"I know," he says resignedly.

His comment makes me laugh, and then I regret that too. Pausing at the bathroom door, I quickly turn back, and the process begins again. "Kill me, Ernie," I whine. I'm sweating now and still unstable. I grab his arm and try leaving the bathroom again.

"You'll be okay. Let's get you into bed."

I make it this time. *Yay me.* I slowly sit down, afraid any sudden movements are going to make me sick again. Like in slow motion, I lower my head to my pillow. Moments later I feel a cool cloth on my forehead. I take in a deep breath and let it out. A slight breeze hits me, and I realize Ernie found one of my fans. The air feels so good. It makes me feel sleepy. Sleep is good. Sleep is all I need.

---

I SLOWLY OPEN my eyes to a dark room. I move my head to the side so I can see out my window. The sky is dark. Did I sleep all day? I sit up slowly and make a note of everything that hurts and things that seem to be better. My head? Still, hurts. My body? Still achy. My stomach? It seems to be on level ground. I don't have the sudden need to race to the bathroom, so I've got that going for me. I turn my body and set my feet onto the ground. I push myself up and pause. Awesome. Still no sign I'm going to get sick. I walk hesitantly out of my bedroom into my living room. The place is dark except for the television. I walk to stand behind the sofa and look down. Ernie's sound asleep on my couch, and one of my favorite classic car restoration shows is playing.

Making my way around the couch, I lift Ernie's feet up and sit, letting his feet rest on my lap. Absently, I run my hands over the top of his feet. I look down and guess he's got size thirteen feet. They're huge. His toenails need to be trimmed, but otherwise, he's got nice feet—well proportioned. Okay, I don't have a foot fetish; I was making an observation about Ernie. I actually know very little about him.

I slide my palm to the bottom of his feet, and he jerks awake, kicking his foot away from me violently.

"Ticklish?"

"Very," he says sleepily.

"Noted."

"How're you feeling?" he asks drowsily.

"Better. How long did I sleep?"

He picks up his phone and then says, "About eighteen hours, give or take."

"Wow! I must have been tired." When Ernie snorts with laughter, I follow suit. "Don't say it. I know I can't handle my liquor."

"It sounds like you handled yours and everyone else's too."

"Don't remind me. I'm never drinking again."

He snorts again, which makes me laugh too. I resume running my hands over the top of his feet and absently make my way up to his lower leg as we watch TV together. Nothing else happens. We sit and watch and talk about the amazing cars. I love it.

# 39

## IT'S TIME

### ERNIE

It's time. The day I donate my bone marrow. The things I had to do leading up to this were more complicated than I thought they would be. I assumed I'd show up, they'd hook me up to a machine, and that'd be it but it's much more than that.

I've had several appointments with the transplant doctors who drew more of my blood for some kind of testing—to make absolute sure I was a match, I guess. I learned that it might hurt and that afterward I might be tired and have some pain. I'll be put under in a surgery setting. I may have to stay the night if I don't handle the process well, but most likely I'll get to go home later today. I'm a pussy when it comes to shit like this, but if I think about Ashley, I stop thinking of myself. She's dealt with far more pain than I'll feel. She's the brave one here.

They told me to be at the surgery center at six in the morning. I wake up at five and shower. Kennedy wakes up at the same time, making coffee and gathering up things to do while I'm having the procedure. My dad is going to meet us at the hospital, and I think I heard Penny say she'd be there too. I'm nervous. I'm not going to lie. This is serious shit. My biggest concern, though, is something going wrong on Ashley's end of this. What if...?

I can't think like that—positive thoughts only.

"Ready?" Kennedy asks.

"Ready."

At the surgery center, I see Dad and Penny already in the waiting room. I sign in, or I guess they call it registering, and wait with my family for my name to be called. In no time, I'm back in the surgery prep area. There they explain to me about anesthesia, the procedure, and recovery. All three of my people are there with me, listening. Kennedy is pretending to be relaxed. Her left eye keeps twitching, which tells me she's nervous. I grab her hand and squeeze it. "This is a piece of cake. Ashley's got the tough job."

When tears slide out of both Kennedy's and Penny's eyes, I smile. "This is the easy part." I'm saying that to reassure them, but it's for me too. A nurse enters the room to add something to my IV, and in minutes it's sleepy time.

Before I know it, I'm awake again. My eyes adjust to the lights around me as I look left and right. On my right, Kennedy stands as soon as she sees me moving around. "How are you feeling?"

"Good. Groggy," I slur the last word.

"You will be for a while longer."

"Do I get to go home today?"

"We haven't heard the final word from the doctors about that. They said it went well and that you did a great job." Her little hands slide down my arm without the IV ports. When she gets to my hand, she takes it in hers and squeezes. "I'm so proud of you, Ernie."

"Thanks, but this was nothing."

She nods. "Your dad wants to see you. I'll send him in."

"Will you come back?"

"Of course. I'll be back after your dad. They want us in here one at a time."

By late afternoon, I've been given the all clear to go home with the warning that I need to take it easy. Dad helps me to Kennedy's truck, and he follows us in his pickup to her place so he can help me get inside and settled. As soon as I get home, I slide right into bed. I'm sore and tired.

Kennedy serves me up some delicious chicken noodle soup while Dad lies next to me on the bed. We've opted to watch some ESPN. None of us are talking about anything important, but I know we're all thinking about Ashley. Her procedure is tomorrow, and we're all going to be there with Penny.

IN THE MORNING, we do a repeat of yesterday, except this time Ashley's step will be done at the hospital instead of the outpatient surgery center because her procedure and recovery are much more complicated than mine. She'll be in the hospital a lot longer and housed in a room with special air filters that are intended to help her avoid infection. In the hospital, they'll be able to keep a close watch on her and her body's reaction to my marrow.

I learned during my information session that the first thirty to one hundred days are critical for Ashley. She'll need to take medications like antibiotics because her immune system will be weak. If the doctors feel she's a high risk for infection, she may have to stay in the hospital for that entire time. This is serious shit.

When we arrive, we see Dad already in the waiting room. "Where's Penny?"

"She's back with Ashley, along with both sets of grandparents. As soon as they take her in, she's coming out here to say hello."

We all sit quietly for almost an hour until Penny finally walks out. "How is she?" my dad asks first.

"She's good. This part of the process isn't as hard as the chemo and radiation she's had the last two weeks." She smiles, but it isn't a real one. She's worried—or maybe scared is a better word. The procedure for Ashley entails giving her my marrow through her central venous catheter, much like a blood transfusion. She'll be awake for her part of the process, so that's why Penny is going back to sit with her.

Penny continues, "Well, I wanted to introduce everyone before I go back in to sit with her." She turns to the three people walking out behind her. "Dad, Tucker, Elaine? Let me introduce you to everyone. This is Ernie. He donated his bone marrow for Ashley."

They all approach me at once, patting my back, shaking my hand, and then Elaine kisses my cheek. "We heard the story. What a wonderful boy," says Elaine. She's been crying, and I'm pretty sure Penny's dad has red eyes as well.

Penny continues, "My mom is back with Ashley. She'll come out when I go back in. She continues with her introductions. "This is Ernie's girlfriend, Kennedy." They all do the same to Kennedy, who takes it in stride. "And this is Donal," she says a little more softly. "Ernie's dad." She looks up at my dad and smiles shyly at him. He looks down at her, doing the same.

Their little flirt fest is interrupted when Penny's dad says, "Donal, you raised a wonderful boy. You've been a good friend and a shoulder for Penny leading up to this. It's nice to finally meet you, son."

I nearly start laughing. *Son?* My dad and Penny's dad are about the same age. They've both got silver hair, although my dad looks good for his age. He's built like the rest of the Flynn men, and thanks to construction work, he's still got muscular arms and a decent upper body. I guess if I were a chick, I'd find him somewhat attractive.

After the introductions, Penny heads back into Ashley's room, and we all sit. I've got Kennedy on one side and Dad on the other. Penny's parents sit side by side, the same with Tucker and Elaine.

"Your dad and Penny?" Kennedy whispers in my ear.

"Apparently." I shrug.

"You okay with that?"

I nod. "Yeah." I'd like to tell you I've got mixed feelings about Dad dating, but I don't. He was a rock for us after Mom died. He's kept her memory alive for all of us, and we all know, without a doubt, that Mom and Dad were soul mates. But that shouldn't mean he can't find happiness with someone else. Maybe she's not the love of his life, but maybe she's someone he could love. I hope it works out for him.

# 40

## WEDDING DAY JITTERS

### KENNEDY

*Why am I nervous?* I'm not the one getting married today. Maybe it's because I'm going to a wedding as Ernie's date—as his girlfriend. I'm not sure I'm ready for it. The Flynn family is a force to be reckoned with on an average day. If they don't like us paired up, I'm sure I'll hear about it at some point today, especially if there's beer involved, and there's definitely beer involved at a Flynn wedding.

When I exit my bathroom, I look up and gasp. "Ernie, you look amazing." He's wearing a black tuxedo with an ivory shirt and a plaid bow tie. I know the tie was a gift from Donal to his sons today. It's made from the Flynn tartan, so the plaid is orange, blue, and brown. The sight before me seriously takes me aback. I've never, in my life, seen a more handsome and sexy man. My first instinct is to tear his clothes off and have my way with him, but we're late. "Later." I give him a hungry look.

"Yeah, definitely. You look fucking beautiful, Kennedy." I look down at my new black dress that I bought the day of our shopping trip.

"Claire helped me pick it out." It's black, of course, but not my usual style. This dress is fitted from the top all the way down to the short hem. It hits me above my knee, but because it's tight, it feels shorter than that. There's pleating, or I guess it's called ruching, at the waist that's all gathered on my left side that makes my waist look much smaller than it actually is. The bodice is off the shoulder, and it has long sleeves that bell at the middle of my forearm and hang to my wrist.

Claire also talked me into buying a silver cuff bracelet and a pair of shoes that look death defying. I refused to try them on until she gave me those sad puppy-dog eyes. Under protest, I agreed to try them on. As soon as I slipped on the silver strappy heels, I was shocked at how comfortable they were. Granted, I only had them on for about fifteen minutes. Several hours in heels is another story completely.

Ernie takes three giant steps until he's standing right in front of me. He slides his hands around my waist and whispers in my ear, "Promise me you'll keep those shoes on when I fuck you sideways tonight."

Okay, on second thought... *Thank you, Claire!* I love these shoes. "I will." I smile up at him.

"Your hair looks pretty too, princess." He picks up a curl and lets it slide through his fingers.

I haven't done much to it. I let it air-dry; then I used a curling iron with a huge barrel on it to create big, soft curls and waves.

"In all my life, Kennedy, I've never seen anyone as beautiful as you."

I suck in a gulp of air. That's such an amazing thing for him to say. "Thank you." I clear my throat. "We'd better get going. We're going to be late."

---

WE'RE LATE. But because the wedding portion of the day is

very relaxed, no one is angry with us. As soon as Donal steps onto the end of the runner, I watch as Ethan moves to stand to his right. He turns to face the back where Ed and Scarlett are standing in front of Ernie and me. When the music starts, I flinch. It's not the typical wedding song. It's more hip-hoppy. I look up at Ernie, confused, but he's got his head thrown back laughing.

"Ernie?" I hiss.

He turns to whisper, "It's M.C. Hammer's 'Here Comes the Hammer.'"

I can't help it; I start to giggle.

When we hear a shriek coming from behind us, I stop laughing immediately. "Ernie Flynn! I'm going to kill you!"

Apparently, Claire doesn't like the song, and neither does Ethan. When I look up to the front of the aisle, he looks like he's about to implode. Suddenly, the music changes, and we hear John Legend's "All of Me." Yeah, that's a much better song.

It's go time. Ernie and I walk slowly up the aisle behind Ed and Scarlett. By the time we're in place, "All of Me" ends and the "Wedding March" begins. We all turn to watch Claire and her dad step into view. I hear Ethan gasp, and I feel Ernie stiffen. As she gets closer, I see her eyes shining with tears. She's smiling and crying. Next, I look over at Ethan who's crying like a baby. It's easily the cutest thing I've ever seen. When Claire gets to him, they fall into each other's arms. They whisper to each other until they burst into laughter.

"Let's get hitched," says Claire happily.

"Definitely." Ethan wipes his eyes and grabs Claire's hand.

Before Donal begins, Claire turns and hands Ernie her bouquet, but before she turns back to Ethan, she glares at Ernie and whispers, "Your ass is mine, fuckface."

Ernie snickers loudly, which makes some of the guests laugh too. Nope, she didn't like that song whatsoever. Scanning the crowd, I see a few faces I recognize and a sea of beautiful people—the Flynns are here, and they take up almost the entire groom's side of the venue.

They're holding the wedding ceremony in the same room as the reception, but the majority of guests won't be here until later. Claire and Ethan wanted the wedding portion to be a more intimate group of family and close friends. So, Flynn intimate still means about seventy-five people. And by the number of tables in the large hall, I'd guess the reception is going to be closer to three hundred people, maybe more.

I return my attention to the ceremony as they're exchanging rings. When Donal says, "You may kiss the bride," I know it's almost over. Ethan and Claire Flynn are introduced to us as they make their way back down the aisle. All seventy-five people clap loudly as they stroll past.

# 41

## THE RECEPTION

ERNIE

With the wedding over and the reception in full swing, I take a minute to reflect. My best friend just married my little brother. Now she's not just my best friend, she's my sister. It fits. Claire and I would never have made it as anything other than friends or as siblings. She wanted more, and I tried, once, but it didn't work. Truthfully, I love her and care about her, but not like *that*—not romantically.

I plop my ass down at a table with a cold glass of beer in my hand. I take a big drink and sigh. "What a week." I think I'm still a little drained from the bone marrow procedure, but not enough to keep me from working Wednesday through Friday right alongside Kennedy. Then, we had the rehearsal shit last night and the wedding today. I could use a nap. Maybe Kennedy and I can lay around in bed all day tomorrow. Sunday's are good for that. Oh, and for football, let's not forget that. Maybe her dick of a brother is playing on television tomorrow. I should check.

"How're you doing?" asks my gorgeous date.

I watch as she sips from her water bottle, and I do my best not to think about her lips around my dick. No beer? She did swear she'd never drink again. "Better now that you're here." I pat my leg, signaling for her to sit on my lap.

"Uh, I'm not sitting on your lap, Ernie."

I look up at her face. "Why not? You sit on me at home." I wink.

"Because I don't want people to worry about me crushing you. At home, I don't care." She smirks back.

"I don't give a fuck what people think. I want to hold you."

She shakes me off. "Maybe later."

I watch her walk away, her round little ass swinging from side to side. That dress is killing me. I reach down and adjust my dick. She makes me hard looking at her.

My thoughts are interrupted by a hard slap on my back. I look to my right to see Wesley Martin. He graduated high school with Ethan and used to hang out at our house a lot. "What's up, Wes?"

He chuckles. "It's a shame."

Okay, I'll bite. "What's a shame?"

"About the bridesmaids."

"What about the bridesmaids?" I'm not going to like this.

"Well, isn't it the rule that, as a groomsman, you end up fucking one of them?"

I *will* be fucking one of them, but I'm not going there. I shrug. "I guess. Where're you going with this?"

"Well...." He chuckles again. "The blonde one is hot as sin, but I saw her slow dancing with another chick. So, she's out."

"Uh-huh."

"And unless you've changed, you're definitely not going to bang the fat one." I start to stand, making a growling sound. The little asshole continues. "Oh, unless you've suddenly become a chubby chaser."

At full height, I'm at least eight inches taller than this little fucker. Taking a calming breath, I speak. "Let me tell you a few things about Kennedy Corcoran."

"She the fat one?"

I don't give a response to that statement because it doesn't deserve one. "She's fucking brilliant. Did you know she's a structural engineer?" I don't wait for him to respond. "She single-handedly oversees some of the commercial projects for my dad. She commands a group of about twenty full-time guys. On top of that, as the general contractor, she deals with the subcontractors too."

"Uh, okay. It doesn't—"

I don't let him speak. "Secondly, she's the most confident, sexy woman I've ever met. I also think she's the most beautiful woman I've ever seen. She's pretty good lookin' too."

"What the fuck, dude?"

"Thirdly." I step into Wes's personal space. "She's *my* woman, and if you ever say another disparaging word about her to me or anyone else, I'm gonna jam my fist so far down your throat you won't be able to speak again. You got me?"

"Your w-woman?"

"She's my woman, and I'm fucking proud to have her on my arm. She takes my breath away." Okay, I said too much there, but it's all true. Every. Fucking. Word.

"Whatever, dude. More pussy for me."

I snort. "Good luck with that, *Frodo*." Too harsh? *Nah.*

"Fuck you, Ernie."

"No thanks."

I sit back down in my seat and breathe deep, attempting to hold back the strong desire to punch that little prick anyway. Just as I'm about to pick up my glass, I feel a soft bottom slide into my lap. "Hey," says my sexy date.

"Hey? Change your mind about my lap?"

"I've changed my mind about a lot of things. I love you,

Ernie. I love you so much." When her lips meet mine, I swipe my tongue as far into her mouth as it will go. I'm rock-hard in seconds, and that's not from her ass on my lap. It's because she loves me. She finally fucking loves me.

I pull away. "I love you too, so much it hurts sometimes," I confess quietly.

"I know. But I've got you now, and you've got me." She kisses me softly.

*Finally.*

# 42

# THE MOMENT I KNEW

## KENNEDY

I've been observing the people at this reception all evening. If you're into people watching, this place is a gold mine. For example, I've seen Claire punch Ernie in the arm right after another M.C. Hammer song blasted from the speakers. I was right there for that one. She nearly knocked him over.

Ernie laughed it off, promising her that there will be "no more M.C. Hammer songs." Apparently, the two of them have had a long-standing battle. Claire's name is Mary Claire Hammer, or M.C. Hammer, like the 80s hip-hop star. Ernie has used it against her for years, and she's over it. I guess he thinks this is his last shot at the joke because she's now Mary Claire Flynn. He's right.

I also watched Ashley's grandparents walk into the room holding a gift in their hands. They went right to Donal, giving him the package. When they saw me, they waved me over as well. "Penny wanted to come too, but she can't leave Ashley right now."

I knew that. Ashley is at high risk of infection, so they're keeping her in a sort of quarantine. It's why we can't see her until she's out of the woods. Penny has been texting Donal with updates, but it's not the same as seeing her for ourselves. Fingers crossed that little girl will be out of the hospital soon and living the life she deserves.

When Ernie sees them, he weaves his way through the crowd to get to them. "How is she?" he asks nervously.

"She's hanging in there. She's a tough little bear," says her proud grandfather.

"She's still pretty weak. She's had the typical reactions to the new bone marrow that they expected, so nothing to worry about," says Barb, adding to her husband's comments.

"Glad to hear that. Would you two like something to eat? Cake?" asks Donal.

"That's very kind, but no, thank you. We wanted to drop off a little gift for the newlyweds. It's from all of us. I'm sure we'll see you all soon." Barb winks at Donal.

As they leave, Ernie leans over to me, holding a large piece of cake. "You didn't have any cake, so I brought you some. I'll go grab you something to drink. Beer?"

"Punch, please." I give him a withering look. "Remember last Saturday?"

"You're never drinking again. I remember."

Sitting at an empty table, I take a bite of my cake. "Mm, good."

Moments later, Ernie has a glass cup filled with punch, a bottle of water, napkins, and a small plate filled with mints and nuts. "I saw these and wasn't sure if you liked mints or nuts, so I got both." He sits next to me. "Do you?"

Ernie is doting on me. It's so damn sweet. "Do I what?" I take another bite of delicious wedding cake.

"Like mints and nuts."

"I like the nuts. I'm not a fan of the mints." As I'm about to take another bite, I ask him, "What about you? Do you like the nuts and mints?"

"Yep, love 'em both, but I prefer the mints," Ernie says, tossing back a couple of the mints. "See? We're a perfect match."

A part of the evening that hasn't been fun watching is the line of women who've been hitting on Ernie. The only good part is watching him ignore them or literally push them away. What's with women today? They're all hands and claws. At one point, he had two women, one on each side, groping him. I'm pretty sure one of them brushed her hand over his dick—on purpose. When that happened, Ernie looked pissed. I didn't hear him, but his words must have been harsh because the girls practically ran away.

Since I was staring at him, it's not surprising that his eyes caught me. When they did, he gave me a big smile and a sexy wink. I smiled back and made my way over to Scarlett and her girlfriend. I don't need to worry about Ernie and those other women. He's here with *me*.

After eating cake, I sit at a table with some of my coworkers. Johnny-cake and his wife are here, as is Dave and his girlfriend. Timmy's here with a pretty date sitting on his lap. Shockingly, I discover she's his fiancée. "How old are you, Timmy?"

"Nineteen."

Wow, that's young to be getting married already, but I smile and congratulate the couple. Good for them. I hope they make it. It makes me think of what happened earlier with Ernie and *his* lap. Now I feel guilty after I rebuked Ernie for asking me to sit on his lap, so much so I get up from the table full of my crew and make my way back to his table to apologize. It's then that I hear it. Every word.

Ernie is talking with a short guy who's blabbering on about the wedding rules and how Ernie gets to "fuck a bridesmaid." I've heard that too. But when I hear the guy refer to me as "the fat one," I stiffen. Ugh, that's so rude. I can't help wondering what Ernie's going say to that? It could be anything. He could agree with him, he could laugh, he could change the subject, or he could defend me. Holding my breath, I listen to my man say the most amazing things about me, really letting that little twerp have it. He not only defended me, he *bragged* about being with me. It's at that exact moment, I know. *I love Ernie Flynn.* Okay, the truth is I've loved him for a while. I couldn't admit it. Loving someone is scary shit. I tried it once. It didn't stick. But this time it's different because I'm in love with Ernie Flynn and he loves me. *All of me.*

After the little jerk walks away, I watch Ernie sit back down in his chair. I take that opportunity to slide right onto this lap. Wrapping my arms around him, I finally say the words. "I love you, Ernie." His reaction is perfect—a deep, sexy kiss and a hard-on right beneath my ass. *God, I love this man.*

# 43

# BEST NIGHT EVER

## ERNIE

When I see my girl is tired, we say our goodbyes to everyone and head home. We're both quiet on the ride, but we're still touching. Her hand is on my thigh; my hand is on top of hers. Kennedy breaks the silence first. "That was a beautiful wedding. Great party too."

"It was. I think everyone had a good time."

"Well, everyone except for poor Ed."

"Poor Ed? Why do you say that?" My big brother prefers to be a stick in the mud.

"Well...." She stops to think. "He sat in the corner."

"He does that. It's typical Ed. What about his best-man speech? Jesus, what was that?"

"About three sentences," Kennedy says, giggling. "Short and sweet."

"I don't think Ethan minded. It's expected of Ed to be succinct."

Kennedy giggles again; then she smiles. "Your speech was perfect."

"Thanks." I didn't let her read it beforehand. I was nervous about having to give the "dude of honor" speech. I didn't need her critiquing it.

"I hope you kept a copy of that. I'd like to reread it."

I pat my breast pocket. "Got it right here, sweet cheeks." I've made her giggle again, and it's such a sweet sound.

By the time I've pulled up to Kennedy's place, she's dozing. "Wake up, sleepyhead. We're home."

She opens her door and starts to step out, but I make it around the front of the car in time to help her. I attempt to pick her up, but she waves me off. "I can walk. Just hold my hand."

I can do that. Inside, I follow her into the bedroom. She strips out of her dress and those fuck-me heels and slips into my tee that she likes to sleep in. I strip down to boxers and follow her into bed. Turning to face me, she says, "I'm too tired for the sexy times tonight."

"Well," I say as I push her hair away from her beautiful face, "I was hoping tomorrow could be a lazy day. You know, sleep in, watch some football, eat comfort food, and later in the day, we can put our wedding clothes back on and do it the way we planned."

"The way we planned?"

"Yeah, with you letting me slowly peel that dress off you and then you wearing only those sexy heels while I do dirty things to you."

"And you only wearing your bow tie?" she says with a giggle.

"If that's what you want. How does that all sound?"

"It sounds perfect. It'll be Sunday Funday."

"Sunday Funday? That's perfect." Then, as I start to get sleepy, I add, "Love you."

Then I hear the five best words in the English language. "I love you too, Ernie."

*Best. Night. Ever.*

# 44

# SUNDAY FUNDAY

## KENNEDY

Why is it on those days when you get to sleep in, you wake up at the ass crack of dawn? I don't have the answer either, but it's vexing. So, instead of sleeping in on our first "Sunday Funday," I wake up with the rooster, as they say. I scoot out from under Ernie's arms and make my way to the bathroom. I've got something important to do first thing today, so I might as well get a jump on it.

When that's taken care of, I tiptoe into the kitchen to make a pot of coffee. I search the fridge for something to make for breakfast, but all I have is orange juice and a tube of those cinnamon rolls that you bake. I guess it's better than nothing. I turn the oven on and pop open the cardboard tube. Laying out all eight circles of dough, I wait for my oven to preheat. Once that happens, I slide the pan into the oven and set the timer.

As I sip my coffee, the smell of cinnamon wafts into the air. I love that smell. It reminds me of Christmas morning and my mom's famous cinnamon pecan rolls. Yum! When the timer bell dings, I slide off my stool at the breakfast bar and pull the rolls out of the oven. The wrapper says to wait to frost them, but I love it when it's all melted on top. Pulling off the tin lid, I spread each roll with as much frosting as possible.

As I ponder whether or not I should eat before Ernie wakes up, I feel big arms wrap around my waist. "What happened to sleeping in?"

"Ugh, I tried, but of course I woke up early."

"I hate when that happens," he says as he kisses my neck.

I stretch my neck out, so he'll do it again. Of course, he does. I moan a little bit when I feel his big hands palm my breasts and his hard erection at my back, and I know what he wants. "I thought we were going to have a matinee."

"Can't we do it more than once today?"

"Uh, yeah." *Duh.*

Grabbing me by the hand, he leads me back into the bedroom. "Let's have shower sex. We've never done that before."

"No, we haven't. It sounds fun." Giggling, I start to pull off my T-shirt as I follow him into the bathroom.

As I have the shirt up around my head, I hear, "What the fuck is this?"

For a split second, I wonder what he's talking about, but then it hits me. I rip the shirt off the rest of the way and stare at the tiny stick in Ernie's hand.

"What is this, Kennedy?"

"It's a pregnancy test."

"It's positive." He looks shocked. "I thought...."

Looking at the pregnancy stick and then at Ernie's stunned face, I feel just a tad nauseous. I've got to keep it together because Ernie looks like he's about to lose it. "Me too. I thought I started my period last weekend, but it never actually started. There was only spotting, so I read some things on the internet that said it's not uncommon to spot if you're pregnant. So, I waited a full week to see if I was just late. When my period never came, I bought a pregnancy test." *Or four.* I point to the one in his hand.

"So... we're pregnant?" he practically squeaks.

I take the stick from him and read the writing. "Yep, it says right here: 'Pregnant.'"

"How accurate are these things?"

"I'd say they were pretty accurate." I reach down and pull open a drawer next to the sink. Sitting in a perfect row inside the drawer are three other pregnancy tests from different manufacturers that I'd taken yesterday. "These are all positive too."

Before I know it, I'm being picked up off the floor and carried back into the bedroom. He lays me gently on the bed. Sliding up next to me, he looks into my eyes. "You're amazing, angel. I'm so fucking happy, Kennedy." He leans in and kisses me softly. Bringing his arms around me, he pulls me closer to his body. "We're having a baby."

"We are. It's scary and exciting."

"Yeah. I know what you mean." We lay like that for a long time, lost in our own thoughts. "I was just thinking...." he says softly.

"About what?"

"That I'll finally be Dad's favorite."

I giggle. "Oh, yeah. How do you figure?"

"I'll be the first one to give him a grandkid. I'm set for life."

I giggle again and kiss his neck. "I guess that's true for me too. This will be Mom and Dad's first too."

"I'm going to be a dad."

"You are. You'll be a great dad."

"Do you think so?" he asks, sounding worried. "I'll never be as good a dad as mine is though."

"Why not?"

"Because. He's the best. No one will ever be better than him."

His sweetness and his heart make me so happy, a few tears escape. "The fact that you recognize what a good dad looks like means that you'll strive to emulate that. You'll be an amazing father, Ernie. I'm excited to share all of that with you."

"Me too." He runs his fingers down my bare back. "You'll be such a good mom too, Kennedy. God, how did I get so lucky? I don't deserve all of this."

"You do. We both do."

"I want to call Dad. Can I?"

"I think we should wait until I go to the doctor. Let's get it all confirmed. I'd like to be sure everything is okay before we tell people."

"You're going to tell your mom, right? She already knows it's a possibility."

"Not until I know everything is fine. I won't put her through that again."

"I get it. Are we at risk of another one of those pregnancies?"

"I'm not sure. We can ask the doctor about that. I'm also worried about the fact that I drank last Saturday night. I want to ask her about that as well, but for now, I only want to think positive thoughts about our child."

"I agree. Let's spend our Sunday Funday thinking good thoughts about our baby and our wedding."

"Wedding?"

"Of course. You think I'm having a baby without getting married to the woman I love?"

"Are you asking me to marry you?"

"I'll ask you when I take you out on our first official date next Saturday."

"Wow, ruin the surprise why don't you."

"The ring will be a surprise." He winks, then pulls me even tighter against him. "I wonder...."

"You wonder? About what?"

"Which will it be?"

"Will what be?"

"Our kid. Will it be Steve or will it be Tina."

I start to laugh so hard tears appear. "You're such a dork. I think we should wait to decide that." When I stop laughing, my stomach growls.

"Oh, I need to feed my pregnant fiancée."

Fiancée? It sounds weird, but I like it. "Yeah, fetch me a cinnamon roll, slave."

Ernie stops midstep. "Wow, that reminds me. Did I ever tell you about my fantasy?"

"A fantasy in which you're my slave?"

"Uh-huh."

"I'm all ears. Tell me more, servant boy."

"Oh fuck. That's exactly what you called me. Servant boy. Oh, and drudge. You demanded I lick your pussy." With his cock hard and pointing my way, he starts to make his way back to me, looking at the apex of my thighs as he licks his lips.

I put my hand up in that stopping motion. "Feed me. *Then* eat me, *drudge*."

"Oh, fuck, Kennedy. I almost came from that." He turns and scurries out the bedroom door. In less than thirty seconds, he's back with a cinnamon roll and a bottle of water. "You eat while I eat," he says huskily.

Kneeling beside the bed, Ernie pushes my legs open wide. I can't eat when this is about to happen, so I just hold onto my breakfast with one hand and grab his hair with my other one. "Get to work, slave."

He licks me from back to front, and I moan loudly. "Such a good boy, Ernie."

He pulls away, looking up a me. "Am I?"

"Hell yeah."

Ernie pulls himself up so we're face-to-face. "Say that again as I'm sliding into you."

As he presses his hard cock into me so slowly it makes me pant, I whisper, "You're my good boy, aren't you, Ernest?"

"Fuck yeah!" he shouts. Then, moaning as he thrusts into me, my man gets to work making Sunday Funday the *Best. Day. Ever.*

45

———————

## IT'S OFFICIAL

KENNEDY

So far, Ernie is doing as I asked. He's keeping the pregnancy news to himself, but it's only been a few days. He went to the OB-GYN with me yesterday for the first visit. He wanted to be there when I got the official results. He also had questions for my doctor.

When the positive results were announced, Ernie and I started hammering Dr. Sinclair with questions. Our biggest concern was about whether or not I could have another ectopic pregnancy. The news was mixed. While I am at a higher risk of having another one, the odds are low. So, we're crossing our fingers and toes and anything else we can cross to make sure that doesn't happen.

I was also told not to worry about the bachelorette party. "Lots of women drink before they realize they're pregnant. Just take good care of yourself and that baby now." She told me to get folic acid and prenatal vitamins and to eat a well-balanced diet. *I hope that includes mac 'n' cheese.*

Ernie wanted to know about heredity and birth weight. Apparently, he and his brothers were ginormous babies.

"Kennedy is small. What if the baby is too big?" *Damn, he's sweet.*

"Well, we'll cross that bridge when we get there, but a C-section is an option. But let's not get ahead of ourselves. We'll schedule a vaginal ultrasound for a month from now so we can see how things are progressing. Sound good?"

What she means by "progressing" is she wants to be sure it's not an ectopic pregnancy. "Yeah. Sounds good."

Before we step out of the office, Ernie turns to Dr. Sinclair. "You know Kennedy is a foreman at a commercial construction site?"

"Oh yeah?" Dr. Sinclair says, sounding surprised. "Good for you."

Ernie ignores the props the doc just gave me. "Well, it's dangerous and...."

"Lots of workplaces are dangerous, Ernie. Being a doctor or a nurse is dangerous." She turns to me, asking, "Do you use safe procedures and wear protective gear?"

"Yes. Of course."

"I think she'll be fine, Ernie. Now, we'll want to revisit this when you're much further along, Kennedy. We can't have your crew worrying more about you than their own safety."

"True. Good point." I get that. My guys will be extra diligent about me when I'm around them. "But, by then, we'll be working inside, so no worries," I say with a smile and a wave.

"That's good." Dr. Sinclair turns back to Ernie. "Don't worry, Ernie. I've got your back. We'll make sure Kennedy is safe. Okay?"

"Yeah, whatever," he grumbles. That was definitely not the answer he wanted. "But, when they paint and shit, you're not going to be there."

"I agree. Those fumes are pretty strong."

"Damn straight." In the car, Ernie has more to say on the

subject. Turning to face me, he clears his throat and says, "You know I think you're amazing on the job, right?"

I nod.

"But that doesn't mean I'm not going to worry. Nothing you say will prevent that from happening. With that said, when I have concerns, I want you to hear me out, and I'll listen when you tell me why I'm wrong, okay?"

I laugh at his last sentence. "Okay." I lean over and kiss his lips. "I'll be careful. I want this baby as much as you do. I won't put her at risk."

"*Her?* You think it's a *her?*"

"I have no idea. It's just a figure of speech. Next time I'll say 'him.'"

"Damn. *A little girl?* Tina Flynn. That sounds good, right?" He puts his car into gear.

"About that—"

Interrupting, he asks, "Can I tell my dad now?"

"Will you ask him to keep it between the three of us for now? You can tell him about my past, uh, issues, if that helps."

"I know the Flynns are a well-oiled gossip machine, but if I ask him, he'll keep it to himself."

"If you're sure, then that's fine." I'm still not telling my mom, not until I know the pregnancy is not at risk.

# 46

# THE PROPOSAL

## ERNIE

I've got it all planned. Sure, Kennedy knows it's coming, but she hasn't seen the ring. The ring? Well, it's special. It was my mom's engagement ring. Before she died, she gave each of us one of her rings. My big brother, Ed, got her wedding band. She gave me her engagement ring, and Ethan got her mother's ring. They were all equally important to her, so she just drew straws to see who got which ring. I haven't looked at mine for eighteen years. It's been in Dad's safety deposit box all this time.

Before I told Dad about the baby, I asked for my—I mean, Mom's ring. It's an emerald. Mom's eyes were green, so Dad chose this ring to match them. I waited in the bank lobby for him to get the ring. When he came out of the vault, I could tell he'd been crying. It's still hard for my dad, even after all these years. I suspect that box holds lots of memories.

When he handed me the little black box, I smiled. "Thanks, Dad. I know that wasn't easy."

"Lots of memories son. Lots of good memories." Slapping me on the back, he added, "I'd be sad if this ring were going to anyone besides Kennedy Corcoran. She's a keeper, Ernie."

"She sure is." I pop open the lid, and the emotion of seeing it again after all this time makes my eyes burn. She never took this ring off—not until the very end. I wipe away my own tears as I pull the emerald Claddagh ring from its perch. The ring is yellow gold with a heart-shaped emerald. There are small diamonds all the way around the center stone. I count twelve diamonds altogether. The gold band isn't wide, but it's thick. I lift the ring to my lips and kiss it. Then I look up and say, "Thanks, Mom."

"Rachel would have loved Kennedy."

"You think so?"

"I know so. She'd be proud of you too, Ernie. You've turned into an extraordinary man."

"Thank you, Pops," I say quietly before looking back up at him. "So, *Grandpa*—" I pause for emphasis. "—what say we go grab some lunch?"

"Sure... uh, what? Did you just call me Grandpa?"

"Did I? Huh, I wonder why."

"Ernie." He grabs my arm to stop me from walking any further. "Don't screw with me. Am I going to be a grandfather?"

I turn to him. "You are. Is that okay?"

"Okay? Okay? Holy shit! I'm going to be a grandfather," Dad shouts loudly. Several people in the bank lobby clap for him. "Jesus," he says, getting emotional again. "I'm going to be a Pop-pop?"

Pop-pop is what we called his dad. "You are, but...."

"There's a but?"

"You can't tell anyone. *Yet.*"

"What? Why not?"

"Let's go grab a burger, and I'll explain."

With Dad's promise to keep our secret, for the time being, my only other job is to plan the most romantic date ever in the history of the world. No problem. I'll just call Claire.

"WHERE ARE YOU TAKING ME?" asks my gorgeous date.

"It's a surprise."

"No hints? None?"

"Nope. Something about tonight has to be a surprise." Squeezing her knee, I look over and watch her bite her nails. She doesn't have much to chew. Working on a construction site makes having fancy nails impossible. My eyes travel down her body, and I smile. She's wearing the same dress as she did at the wedding. I had to return my tux, so I'm wearing a dark charcoal gray suit with a blue shirt and a blue and gray paisley tie. I look damn good but not near as good as my woman.

When I pull up to our construction site, Kennedy turns. "Did you forget something at work?"

"Nope."

I hop out of the car and run to her side. I open the door and hold my hand out for her. When she takes it, I pull her along until we're inside the building. The interior is starting to come together. The windows are in and the doors are now in place. There's no electricity, but we don't need any.

Opening the main door, I hold it open for her. When she steps inside, she gasps. "Ernie? Did you do all of this?"

"Maybe." Inside I've set up a small table with a tablecloth, nice dishes, and glasses. Candles light the entire area. I've got a bottle of sparkling cider chilling and a chafing dish keeping our food warm.

Giggling, Kennedy makes her way to the table. "Why here?" she says, looking up at me.

"Because this was where I first saw you. You were pissed as hell at me. Your hair was wild, and your eyes practically glowed. In all my life, I'd never seen anything as beautiful as you that day. You took my breath away. I was a goner from that moment on. So, I thought this would be the perfect place."

She smiles shyly at me. "Ernie, that's so sweet." Pushing herself up to her tiptoes, she kisses my mouth.

"You hungry?"

"I am. I wasn't on the way over because of nerves, but now that we're here, my appetite is back."

I pull her chair out for her and wait until she's seated and help scoot her close to the table. I walk over to the chafing dish and pull the lid open like a real waiter. "Ta-da!"

She covers her mouth with her hands as she giggles. "Is that mac 'n' cheese?"

"It is. Homemade. Your mom's recipe."

"My mom's? She knows?"

"She knows. So do your brothers. They wanted to kick my ass, but your mom told them to 'shut the hell up.'"

Kennedy practically cackles at that. "Damn, I wish I'd seen that."

"Yeah, it was pretty cool."

I pour her a glass of sparkling cider and offer her water as well. Then I place a small salad in front of her and dish her up some "cheesy goodness," as Kennedy likes to call it.

"This is so perfect. Perfect for us, Ernie."

Smiling, I sit across from her. I'm not a bit hungry. My nerves are playing havoc with my stomach. Until she says "yes" and she's got my ring on her finger, I won't be able to eat. So, I watch her eat instead.

"You're not eating?"

"Not yet."

She sets her fork down and smiles at me. "Okay, I'm ready."

I stand up and move to her side of the table. She turns her body to face me. Kneeling in front of her, I pull the black box from my pocket. "Kennedy Corcoran...." I look up at her to see the most beautiful smile on her face. "God, I love you so much. I didn't think it was possible to be this happy." I watch as a tear slides down her beautiful face. "Please don't cry."

"Happy tears. Don't worry. Keep going."

I pop open the little black box and look down. "This was my mom's engagement ring."

When Kennedy gasps, I look up and see her cover her mouth again. "Ernie?"

"She told me to give this to my true love. You're it, Kennedy. I wouldn't give this ring to anyone else but you." I pull the ring out of the box and hold it in front of her. "Kennedy Corcoran, will you marry me?"

"Yes! Of course."

When I slide the ring onto her finger, it's a perfect fit. That was one thing I hadn't even considered—whether or not the ring would fit. I just assumed it would, and I was right. As I stand up, I pull her up with me. Wrapping my arms around her, I pull her into a kiss. "Thank you. You've made me so happy, princess."

I kiss her long and deep until my stomach growls. "Now I can eat." We sit down at the table and eat and talk. Every once in a while, she holds her hand in front of her and smiles. "The ring, it's perfect. Are you sure Donal doesn't mind?"

"She gave that ring to me before she died. We each got one. Ed got her wedding band, Ethan her mother's ring, and this was mine." I nod toward her hand.

"I'm speechless."

Me too, so I just smile and reach my hand out to hold hers— the one with my ring on her finger, right where it belongs.

At home, I do the thing I wanted to do the night of Ethan's wedding. I slowly peel that sexy dress down Kennedy's body until she's only wearing a lace bra with no straps and matching panties. Making short work of those, I walk her backward until her legs hit the mattress. As she sits, I pulled off the fuck-me shoes. "I thought you wanted to fuck me in those," she asks, confused.

"I do. But I'm not going to fuck you."

"Huh?" she says in a whiny voice.

"Nope. Tonight, I'm going to make sweet, sweet love to my fiancée."

"Sweet, sweet love?"

"That's right, angel. Sweet, sweet love." And that's exactly what I do. Twice.

# 47

# SO MUCH TO DO

## KENNEDY

Well, Donal kept his mouth shut for one entire month, but when I got the news that my pregnancy was not ectopic, there was no holding him back. The idea of being a grandfather must appeal to Donal a great deal because he's told everyone—even strangers.

Ernie and I told my parents together. Dad was shocked; Mom wasn't. They're both thrilled. Mom was relieved when I told her things were looking good. I still worry, but I think that's what mothers do, they worry.

One thing I expected—and got—was the stupid alpha male bullshit from Donal, Ed, Declan, and Keith, Ernie's cousin. They made a huge deal out of me working on the site while I carried their "kin." *Ugh.* I promised them I'd sue if they pushed the thing they're calling "concern" too far, telling him, "I don't care if you're my soon-to-be father-in-law, Donal. I'll sue your ass if you pull me off this job before I'm ready."

"Sweetheart, I'm not doing any such thing. I just want you to know that if and when you decide you want to do a different job within the company, you have my blessing, and you'll have my help. Okay?"

"Okay," I grumbled. I'm not sure I believe him, but there's nothing else I can do about it.

The truth is, there are days when I'd like nothing better than to be sitting in an office. The days the morning sickness is bad is one example. Another is when I'm just too tired to think. Having a baby is hard work, people. It draws everything we have in our bodies to create this life. It's not for wimps. That's for sure.

On top of that, Ernie and I are planning a wedding. We argued for two weeks about what we wanted to do. Ernie wanted to fly to Vegas and get married right away. I knew my parents would be upset about that. They wanted me to wear a big white dress and walk down the aisle at our church. To compromise, we decided to do exactly the same thing Ethan and Claire did. We even chose the same venue and caterers.

As luck would have it, they had a cancellation on Christmas Eve. Ernie was a little apprehensive about getting married on a holiday, but I love the idea. I love Christmas. Although, I hate the idea of all the people who now have to work on that day, but the party planner assured us that, if we didn't get married then, someone else would.

The wedding dress is another problem. I'll be several months along by then, and I have no idea what I'll look like. I make an appointment at a wedding dress shop that specializes in extended bridal sizes; I take my mom and Claire with me. Ashley and Penny come along as well since Penny is one of my maids. Ashley is feeling better, and she's agreed to be my flower girl.

Thankfully, Ashley responded well to the transplant. The doctors are optimistic. She'll have more tests in the coming months, but she's already gained weight, and her energy levels are improving every day. When I asked her if she'd be my flower girl, she jumped up and down excitedly.

At the bridal store, I'm able to look through an entire room full of dresses. The problem is, I need one in a hurry, so I can either buy a sample dress—one off the rack—or have one rushed. As luck would have it, they have a beautiful dress in the back room that had been ordered but never picked up. It's my size; plus it has a lace-up back, so if I gain weight before the wedding, I can loosen those right up. Another bonus is the price. I only have to pay for the remaining balance.

The gown is a strapless A-line style with ivory lace over an ivory skirt. Sewn on top of the lace are clear beads and sequins as well as tiny pearls. There is some bling at the natural waist that actually make me look smallish there. I feel beautiful in the dress; I feel bridal, and I know Ernie will love it.

Since I plan to wear flats with the dress, it needs alterations. Their seamstress in house pins the dress on the spot. At the same appointment, I choose a veil and a sparkly accessory for my hair. The entire bridal experience takes less than an hour. It was meant to be.

After that we go in search of a dress for Claire and Penny to wear. We choose a simple dress in maroon for my two maids. For Ashley, we let her pick any dress she wanted, so she chose one that looks a lot like mine—a pretty ivory dress with lace and beading. It's perfect.

After that, Ashley and Penny head for home so Ashley can rest. Mom, Claire, and I go grab some lunch and do some additional planning. Thankfully, the planner at the venue has the wedding under control. We told her what we wanted, and she promised to deliver.

"So, Penny and Donal?" asks my mom curiously.

"Apparently. He's been there for her since the bone marrow transplant."

"Isn't he about the same age as her parents?"

"Yeah, but Donal's hot," Claire says before shoving a bite of salad into her mouth.

I laugh. "He is."

My mom adds with a hiss, "Oh *yeah*, he is."

That makes both Claire and I break out into giggles. "Mom! You're married."

"So is she," she says, pointing her thumb at Claire. "And you might as well be, honey."

It's true. The day after he proposed, Ernie moved all of his stuff over to my place. Well, not all of it. He left most of his furniture and listed his place for rent as a furnished apartment. According to him, he'll get more rent that way. He must have been right because he had it rented in less than a week for an insane amount of money. Who knew? Well, Ernie. He knew.

# 48

# TIME TO GET HITCHED

## ERNIE

"Can you believe it?" asks Ethan. He's standing behind me, adjusting his bow tie in the full-length mirror.

I swallow hard. "No, I can't. I'm nervous as fuck. What if she doesn't show up?"

"She's already here. The girls all got here about twenty minutes ago."

I turn and stare at my little brother. "Why didn't you tell me?" I growl.

"I didn't realize you were worried. Did you do something to piss her off?"

"No." I look down at my hands then back up to him. "I don't think so."

Patting me on the shoulder, Ethan says reassuringly, "I'm sure you didn't. She's here. She's ready to marry you. God knows why, but she is."

"Because she loves me." I blink a few times. "I can't believe it, but she does."

Ethan's face softens. "She loves you, man. You're both, or I should say, all three of you are going to be very happy."

Sucking in a lung full of air, I look around. "Where's Ed?"

"Who knows? The guy's been flaky as shit lately. He has been ever since he got back from his 'mini' vacation," he says, using air quotes around "mini." "Who goes on vacation by themselves? And for only two days?"

"Ed," we say simultaneously.

"What do you mean by flaky?" I ask.

"Claire says he's all messed up over a girl."

"No way! I thought he was gay."

Ethan throws his head back and laughs. "You douche. You did not."

"Nah, but he hasn't had a girlfriend in...." I look up at Ethan. "Has he ever had a girlfriend?"

"Not that I recall."

"Jesus, I'm surprised his dick hasn't fallen off." I wince. That'd suck.

"Maybe it has. You should ask him." Ethan snickers.

"No way. Not today. Today is all about my bride." *My wife.*

"You boys ready to go?" asks my dad as he walks into our dressing room.

*No!* Jesus, no one told me how scary this shit would be. "Yeah, I'm more than ready." Might as well pretend I'm not a pussy. "Where's Ed?"

"He's already out there. Let's go."

Dad is performing the ceremony for us too. He says he plans to marry all three of his sons. Good luck getting Ed down the aisle. That's never going to happen.

Standing at the altar, I keep my head down, but I angle it slightly so I can see who showed up for this shindig. By the looks of it, everyone did. We invited the Flynns, of course. The Corcorans aren't a small group by any means, so her side is full of them. Plus, every guy on our crew and their dates are sitting back there, watching. I look up and see J.C. smiling at me. He winks, and I smile back. The old coot knew Kennedy was my girl before I did.

I turn and look back at Ethan and Ed. Ethan looks cool and calm, while Ed.... Well, Ed looks like he's ready to puke. I whisper back, "What the fuck, Ed? You hungover or something?"

He glares at me. "No! I'm fine. Just focus on your *own* damn wedding, Ernie," he spits. He emphasizes "own," which is kind of weird.

When the music starts, I quickly turn so I can face the back of the aisle. I blink a few times because the music isn't what we planned, but I've heard it before. Just as I realize what it is, I see Claire at the end of the aisle walking slowly up to the altar with a smirk on her face. She must have bribed the deejay to play "Rubber Ducky." It was Ernie's song on Sesame Street.

When I hear Ethan behind me sniggering, I know he was in on it. I throw my head back and laugh. She got me. When she gets about two feet away, she whispers, "Ha! Got you back, fuckface!" Then she cackles. By now, most of the people know our deal, so they laugh too.

I watch Penny walk toward me holding little Ashley's hand. I could actually cry just from the sight of her today. She looks beautiful. Her blonde hair is starting to grow back. She's smiling and happy as she tosses out flower petals while skipping up the aisle.

When the music changes, I stand straight as a board. I see her dad first; then I see her. *Kennedy.* I nearly choke as I suck in a gulp of air. As she walks toward me, her eyes are on me—only me while mine are only looking at her. Jesus, she's so fucking beautiful.

A sob escapes me, and I can't control it. I think I've been holding in all of these emotions a bit too long because I'm embarrassing my family and myself right now. But when I see

Kennedy crying too, I know it's okay and that I shouldn't give two shits what anyone thinks. This is the most important day of my life—so far. I'm allowed to express my feelings.

When she gets to me, she wraps me in her arms. "You're doing great, Ernie," she says, sniffling. "I'm so excited to marry you," she whispers.

I whisper back, "Me too, princess. You're breathtaking, Kennedy. There'll never be a bride as stunning as you."

"Thank you. You look hot too."

I chuckle in her ear, and she giggles into mine. "Let's do this," she says, pulling away but holding onto my hand.

"Yeah, let's do this."

So, yeah, we did it. After our PG-13 kiss, my dad announces, "Ladies and gents, I'd like to introduce you to Ernie and Kennedy Flynn!" The place erupts into applause. Some of the women are crying while some are just smiling. I think even Carter Corcoran is cracking a smile. Clinton and Johnson? Not so much. That's okay; they'll learn to love me. Everyone does.

"Well, readers, that's our story. I've got to say, it was way better than the previous book about my best friend and my dickhead little brother. Plus, the hero in this tale is much hotter." I feel a jab to my side and wince. My wife just elbowed me in the ribs. Hard.

"They don't want to hear about you, Ernie. They want to hear about the baby and how everything turned out, not about your inflated ego." Kennedy Flynn sighs. "So do you want to talk or should I?"

"You do it. I'll jump in when necessary," adds Ernie, who's lying on the bed, hands behind his head, feet crossed.

"Fine. Okay. Here goes." Kennedy takes a deep breath. "It's a girl!" she squeals.

"She's beautiful," interjects Ernie. "Just like her mama."

"Well, except she's got blue eyes."

"Those could change. You heard the doctor. It could take six months or more for her eye color to change."

"*If* they're going to change, I'm fine with her having your eyes, Ernie. You've got beautiful eyes."

"They'll change, Kennedy. She's your mini me."

"I don't know why you think you know that shit. Anyway," Kennedy sighs, "Rachel Fey Flynn was born on June 21st."

"She wouldn't let me name her Tina for Tina Fey, so we compromised. Actually, I love that she's named after my mom. When I asked my brothers and dad if they were okay with that, they all hugged me and said they loved the idea. Dad said, 'The firstborn granddaughter *should* have her name. It's right and fitting.'"

"That was an emotional conversation," says Kennedy before she kisses Rachel's lovely cheek. "So, um, she weighed... wait for it... nine pounds, fifteen ounces. Thank you very much, Ernie Flynn."

I wince thinking about what it'd feel like to push something that size out of me. No thanks. "Needless to say, Kennedy had to have a C-section. My baby girl was big and healthy. She was also twenty-one inches long.

"I hope that means she'll be tall. Being short sucks."

"Short girls are cute," Ernie says, winking at his wife.

Rolling her eyes Kennedy continues, "Life has been pretty damn good for us, hasn't it, Ernie?"

"It has."

"I haven't gone back to work yet. Ed took over my project in the middle of my eighth month when my blood pressure started to get all wonky."

"Doctor's orders," murmurs Ernie.

"Doctor's orders," mumbles Kennedy. "Actually, I was all right with it. I missed the guys and the job, but my first priority was making sure this little one was born healthy."

"You did a great job, princess."

"Thanks, Ernie," Kennedy says, smiling at her husband. "You're a wonderful father too, babe."

"I know." Ernie snorts out a laugh, which makes Rachel startle in Kennedy's arms.

"You scared her, dork."

Ernie reaches for his daughter. Holding her close to his chest, he coos, "I'm sorry, Pooh Bear. Daddy didn't mean to scare you." He kisses her forehead then lays her on his chest. "Life doesn't get much better than this, does it, Kennedy?"

"Nope. No, it doesn't."

"It's not a bad gig," adds Ernie.

"What's not a bad gig?" my wife asks touching our baby girl's head.

"Being Kennedy's," Ernie says, smiling at his wife.

"And Rachel's. Don't forget Rachel's."

"Never," Ernie agrees. "Definitely not a bad gig at all."

BOOKS BY KAYT MILLER

## **The Palmer Sisters**

Lainie

Agatha

Sadie

Cortland

Keely

Violet

Molly

## **Standalones**

The Art of the Game

The Virginia Chronicles

One of a Kind

The Portrait Painter

Game Changer

Bedhead

It's All Thanks to Santa

Coming Soon: Farm Boy

Coming Soon: Redhead

## **The Flynns**

Out of the Blue

Mick'sology

Vested Interest

The Importance of Being Ernie

The Importance of Being Kennedy's

Quirky Girl

**For a complete list of Kayt's books, visit:**

**Kayt's Website**: kaytmiller.com

## ACKNOWLEDGMENTS

Thank you to Virginia from Hot Tree Editing for editing this book from start to finish.

And an extra special thank you to Becky at Hot Tree Promotions for your advice, expertise, and her positivity.

And to my beta readers. Your feedback is essential to this process. Thank you!

*Many thanks and adoration to Colleen Galligan for re-designing the The Flynn series for me. She read the books twice to get them just right. Thank you, Colleen!*
*To reach Colleen: galligancolleen@gmail.com*

*<3 KM*

# ABOUT THE AUTHOR

How did it all start? Well, I love reading and one day I was searching for a book. A book about a certain type of woman and a specific kind of man and I couldn't find it so, I wrote it. I called it Game Changer and it couldn't have been a more appropriate title. It changed my life in many ways. While my real job is teaching young people, my fun job is conjuring up characters and situations to write about.

My goal, as a writer, is to write stories that relate to all of us, to make readers laugh and maybe cry sometimes. I hope my readers can escape into a fantasy, one that's actually possible. Sure, some of the stories could be dubbed "Insta-love" stories but that's okay. I fell in love with my husband pretty damn fast and with my daughter the second I saw her. So, it's a thing, I swear.

Please Follow Me on these social media sites. Following on BookBub to learn about special book deals.

I love hearing from you!

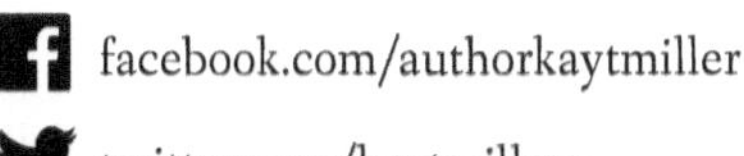
facebook.com/authorkaytmiller

twitter.com/kaytmiller1

instagram.com/kaytmiller1

bookbub.com/profile/kayt-miller

Thank you so much for reading Kennedy and Ernie's story! When I start a story, it begins with an outline, notes, and lots of crazy thoughts running through my head. When I actually start writing, the characters take over, leading me through the story like they're holding my hand—guiding me. The process is exciting and cathartic. With that said, I hope you enjoy the story.

If you did, please go to my website, www.kaytmiller.com, and join my newsletter so you can be the first to know what's coming up next. And...

*Please, leave a review!*

# SNEAK PEEK: QUIRKY GIRL

## THE FLYNNS BOOK SIX

## Chapter 1

*Ed. My Little Brother's Wedding*

Just thirty more minutes and I can get out of here. I've done my big, brotherly duty today so now I'm free to go home, drink a beer, and watch baseball or something mindless that requires no effort on my part to enjoy.

All in all, the wedding turned out pretty good. My speech at the beginning of the reception was short and sweet, emphasis on short. Everyone has eaten, had cake, and now they're on the 'get drunk and dance' portion of the night, and that scene's not for me.

From my spot in a dark corner of the ballroom, I can observe everything that's happening around me. Ethan and Claire had their ceremony and reception in the same room. Not a bad idea, really. If I were to ever marry, I'd do something like this. I scoff aloud. *Who the hell am I kidding?* I'll never get married. Too much can go wrong with a marriage, or fuck, even a relationship.

Not only do fifty percent of marriages end in divorce, a bunch more end when one of the pair keels over. No thanks. The odds for a long, happy marriage are definitely not in my favor. I'm so sure of these facts that I haven't even dated anyone seriously. Ever. I've had a few short-term flings, sure, and my share of one-night stands, but nothing serious. I can't risk it. Too many people count on me. I need to keep my head on straight.

I sigh looking around the room again. So far, no one has punched anyone else, and I've seen no cat fights or other signs that things are getting out of hand. That doesn't mean there won't be because there's about a one hundred percent chance one or more of the Flynn's will do something to turn this nice reception into a barroom brawl. I'll blame the Irish in all of us—it's inevitable.

I scan the room again looking for my dad. When I spot him sitting at a table with his brother, Declan, our eyes meet. He smiles and nods at me, and I do the same. Dad knows me better than anyone. He gets I'm a loner and that I hate shit like this so when it's time for my Irish goodbye, he won't be surprised I'm gone. It won't bother anyone else either—no they won't care. With the wedding done, my role as my baby brother, Ethan's, watchdog and protector is essentially over. Now that he's a married man, he's on his own. Next will be Ernie, my middle brother. That's a shock to my system. I never thought Ernie would settle down. And the woman he fell for is so far removed from his usual bimbos. Kennedy Corcoran is a great girl. Smart, funny, tough as nails. and not afraid of anything. Maybe that's why it works. She doesn't put up with Ernie's shit.

I'm momentarily distracted when the song changes to an M.C. Hammer song, and I watch Claire, my new sister-in-law, take a swing at Ernie. His head is thrown back in a laugh. Ethan looks pissed, and Kennedy seems confused. I'd say Claire was teasing but she just made contact with Ernie's shoulder and it looks like it was hard enough to knock the big oaf off balance. He caught himself before he fell. It didn't stop him from wrapping his arms around the new Mrs. Flynn in a hug. Crisis averted. It looks like the newest Flynn has a good right hook. Noted.

My eyes look to the left at the bar. There's a line of about fifteen people waiting to get their free drinks thanks to the open bar. I pick up my glass of Guinness and sip. I'm only having the one drink. I need a clear head. Why? No reason. I just like to be in control in case someone needs me. My eyes travel further right, and I spot the waitress that keeps grabbing my attention. Mind you, not for a good reason. This girl should *not* be waiting tables. I've watched her elbow my Aunt Marge, my mom's sister, in the arm and press her boobs, what there is of them, into the side of my cousin, Mick's, head as she reached for his empty glass. She's broken at least one glass and a plate, and she's not even gotten to this side of the room yet.

I look at her from head to toe and wince. Her hair is... I'm not even sure I can describe it accurately. It's blondish. I guess you could call it dirty, strawberry blonde. There seem to be different colors of blonde, red, and brown running through it, but that's not the part that stands out. It's the fact that she's got it wadded up into a ball on the top of her head and pieces are sticking out all over the place. Some pieces are sticking straight up, some in her eyes, and others are pointing out on either side of her head. It's like she fixed her hair and then found herself in a category four hurricane on the way to work and left it that way.

Scanning her body from head to toe, I wince again. Her uniform is tight. It's way too small for a girl with her kind of body. She's all ass and thighs. The black skirt she's wearing barely covers her round bottom as it is. She's paired the skirt with a blouse that's at least two sizes too small. Then, she's wrapped up the entire thing with white knee-high socks like the one's Catholic girls wear and dark Converse tennis shoes. Ordinarily, I'd say that look was hot but not on this girl. Not tonight.

When she turns in my direction, I get a look at her face. Pretty—at least the parts that aren't covered by hunks of loose hair. I can see one big eye and a cute little nose as well as full lips that she's painted bright pink. As she approaches my table, I lean back into the shadows. She's picking up plates, silverware, and water glasses and piling them on top of each other. It's too much to carry all at once. When she lifts the pile, several pieces of silver slide off the top and onto the floor. "Shoot!" she hisses. Setting down the things in her arms, she turns away from me and bends down to pick them up.

I blink twice as she bends over because her skirt rises up and up and up until I see most of her Wonder Woman underwear. The panties are blue with white stars all over them and smack dab in the center of her ass is the Wonder Woman logo. I let out a snort of a laugh, which startles her. The forks, spoons, and knives she's holding fly into the air. I watch them scatter around her. When she turns in my direction I say, "You're not very good at this, are you?"

"Huh?" she says blinking her long eyelashes at me.

"Waitressing. You're not good at it."

"Uh, I, uh, I don't know."

"Well, I can tell you, you *aren't*."

I stare at her face watching as her chin begins to quiver. Then she licks those full lips and bites her bottom one. She sniffles, and she lets out a sob. "It's, I'm not bad at it. It's just..." she sniffles again, "...it's the anniversary of Mr. Nibblesworth's death."

"Mr. Nibblesworth?" Who the fuck is Mr. Nibblesworth?

She sobs louder. "My c-c-cat. Mr. Barnabus Nibblesworth. He d-d-died s-s-six months ago t-t-today. I c-can't concentrate.

All I can do is th-th-think about my big fuzzy buddy. Oh, God..."
Her sobs turn into a full-on crying jag in a matter of seconds.
She leaves everything on the table and floor and runs away
weaving in and out of the sea of round banquet tables tripping
and nearly falling at one point.

"Shit." I slowly stand and walk in the direction she ran all
the while muttering, "Not my finest hour making the weird
waitress cry." When I find her, she's still making noises like
she's sobbing. She's putting dirty dishes into one of those
plastic bins that go back to the dishwashing area. I clear my
throat. Not knowing what to say I go with, "Uh, miss? I'm
sorry... about your cat." However, I'm *not* sorry I pointed out
her obvious lack of waitressing skills. Someone needed to
tell her.

She whirls around like a tornado and throws her arms
around my neck. "Oh, you're so sweet. I'm the one that's sorry.
I'm a blubbering crybaby, I was trying *soooo* hard not to cry
tonight."

I feel the back of my shirt grow increasingly wetter. I look
over my shoulder and see a wine glass in her hand that's now
facing downward—remnants of red wine still in the glass. I peer
further down and realize I look like I've just been murdered.
Great.

"Look, I'm sorry about your uh, loss."

She presses her face into my neck, and several strands of her
unruly hair end up in my mouth. I feel her head nod up and
down and the scent of her hair finds its way into my nostrils.
Sweet and tropical. Coconut? Not only that. I believe I feel hard
nipples pressing into my chest. "You're so nice," she says as she
pulls away from me. With her hands now resting on my chest
she looks up at me, smiles, and blinks rapidly. "Wow, you're
really good looking."

"Uh, thanks?" I look down at her and can't help noticing her shirt is gaping open at the top. I do my best not to look, but I can't help it. I'm a guy, and there are nipples in my line of sight.

"Not as good looking as the groom, though. He's a fox."

I blink and look at her when I hear her. "A fox?" She thinks Ethan is a fox?

"Yeah, and the other guy in the tuxedo. He's hotter than you too. But, you're very good looking."

Ernie. She's talking about Ernie now. "Great. Thanks." Jesus, was that supposed to be a compliment? I look down her shirt again. I can't help it. Jesus, I haven't seen a chest that flat since I accidentally saw Karen McCormick's boobs in sixth grade. She dove into the pool, and when she came up for air, she was topless. I recall at the time being quite aroused at the sight, but these bee stings, not so much.

"Eyes up here, please." She says pointing to her face. She's got a smirk on her lips like she thinks she caught me stealing a peek. It was an accident. Believe me. "My name's Beatrice, but I mostly go by Bea so, yeah." She pauses, "What's your name?"

Her eyes are glistening with unshed tears. "Uh, Ed."

"Ed? Not Edward? Eddie? Ooh, I know, *Eduuuaaarrrd-ddooo*. That's sexy. You should definitely go by Eduardo."

"No. It's just Ed."

"Do you like dolphins, Eduardo?"

"Dolphins?" Wow, she changes subjects fast.

"Yeah. Do. You. Like. Dolphins?" she says rolling her eyes like I'm the idiot here.

"I guess."

"Well, I *looovvveee* dolphins. Have you ever been to Shedd Aquarium?"

"When I was twelve."

"Well, I *love* Shedd aquarium. I try to go as often as possible. They have this dolphin show there that is Out. Of. This. World. If I could get a do-over, I'd totally become a dolphin trainer.

Once she's finished with that speech, I reach up and pull her hands away from my chest. "Well, since you seem to be okay, I'd better get back..."

"Give me your phone."

"Excuse me?"

"Give me your phone," she says holding her palm out to me.

I have no idea why I do it, but I pull it out of my back pocket and hand it to her. I watch her program her number on my phone and then stare as she sends herself a text. Great. She's got my number.

"Okay, I'm going to call you later."

"Why?"

"To set up a time to meet."

"Meet?"

"At Shedd. Duh!"

"I don't..."

"If you haven't been there since you were twelve, you're going to be b-l-o-w-n, blown away by it now. It's so amazing. She turns to walk around me, "Okay. Talk to you later," she says waving her pink-tipped fingernails at me.

As I watch her go, I mutter, "What the fuck just happened?"

---

Flopping down onto my couch, I grab the remote for my television. Finally. I'm home. I was able to sneak out of the reception without anyone seeing me. Well, someone probably saw me, but they didn't try and stop me. My family knows me.

"Let's see what's on tonight." Raising my legs, I rest them on my reclaimed wood coffee table and take a pull of my beer. Now, I can finally relax after a long day of family shit. Not that I mind my family shit. I don't. I love my dad and my brothers. It just gets to be overwhelming sometimes——the fact that I need to watch out for them twenty-four-seven takes its toll. I rest my head on the back of my couch and change it to a rerun of one of my favorite movies. I've seen it so many times over the years; I could probably recite the dialogue verbatim. Deciding to search again, I press a few buttons on the remote in search of a baseball game.

Just as I'm about to tune into a baseball game, my phone rings. I groan loudly as I reach in front of me to pick up my phone from the coffee table. I don't recognize the number, but I answer it anyway, "Hello."

"Eduardo?"

I pause. Maybe if I pretend I'm not here, she'll go away.

"Eduardo?"

"It's Ed."

"Eduardo? It's me, Beatrice. Remember? We met at that hot guy's wedding."

"It was two hours ago. Of course, I remember."

Maybe she doesn't understand sarcasm because she just ignores my comment saying, "So, I was just calling to get our ducks in a row about tomorrow."

"Tomorrow?" *Ducks in a row?* Who says that shit?

Paying no attention to my question she keeps going, "Let's meet promptly at nine o'clock outside next to the fountain with the man holding the fish. I'll wear a flower in my hair, so you can recognize me. Okay? Don't be late! Sunday's are a nightmare at Shedd. Okay, bye!" she says in an overly happy and annoyingly chipper voice.

I don't get a chance to reply because she's already gone. "Hello?" She hung up. I hold my phone out in front of my face and stare at it wishing that last two minutes didn't happen. "I'm not going to damn Shedd Aquarium with a girl who's obviously got a screw loose." I should just call her back. But then what? She'd just ramble on and on; not paying one bit of attention to what I'm saying. "Aw hell. I don't have time for this." I toss the phone back onto the table and let my head drop onto the back of my sofa with a groan. "Once. I'll play along once. After that, I'm abso-fucking-lutely shaking this chick off." Definitely. Letting her loose.